Macramé

Incredible Patterns and Project Ideas

LUCY LEONARD

Table of Content

Introduction

When most people think about macramé, they imagine hippies and plant hangers and also have summer camp memories, when they were first introduced to the knotting technique, also known as macramé. "Oh, I remember the macramé," they say. I did that when I was young, "or," My mother used to do that. "Yeah, there's more to macramé than that — lots more. Over many, many years, Macramé has been running here. The technique of knotting arose first in the Middle East as a way to make nets and decorate the edges of cloth. Sailors developed these in their voyages, and macramé spread throughout the world through travel, trade, and the invasion of distant lands. During the Victorian era, it had its heyday, when the craft was highly known. Most people today recall the 1970s macramé, but it was far from the beginning. Our goal in the making Mod Knots was to upend what is nearest to macramé. We'll begin by showing you all the basic knots, step by step, and introduce you to the most commonly used materials, such as cotton, linen, and nylon cord — and then to some not so common ones, including hand, spun wool, soft leather lace, and even wire. Then we'll start designing jewelry. You could never have dreamed of macramé that you might do. In making one-of-a-kind necklaces, bracelets, earrings, and even jewelry collections, we can mix fabrics in unexpected ways and merge macramé with a range of other jewelry-making techniques using Boho-chic designs, such as wire binding, bead stringing, and even metal clay and leatherwork. We will also produce items such as belts and handbags and even a guitar case, as well as a few wearables, including a halter-top and a light variegated wool scarf. So cute! Yet that is not the macramé of your mum. With this versatile (and fun) craft, we hope those new explorations in macramé will inspire your own future adventures.

Chapter 1: Introduction to Macramé

When most people think about macramé, they imagine hippies and plant hangers and have summer camp memories when they were first introduced to the knotting technique known as macramé. "Ah, I know the macramé," they say. I did that when I was young, "or," My mother used to do that. "Yeah, there's more to macramé than that lots more. For many, many years, Macramé has been running here.

The technique of knotting arose first in the Middle East as a way to make nets and decorate the edges of cloth. Sailors developed these in their voyages, and macramé expanded across the world through flight, commerce, and the invasion of distant lands. In the Victorian ages, it had its heyday, when the craft was highly known. Many people today recall the 1970s macramé, but it was far from the beginning. Our goal in the making Mod Knots was to upend what is closest to macramé. We are going to begin by showing you all the simple knots, step by step. We will introduce you to the more widely used fabrics, including hemp, linen, and nylon cord — and then to some not so popular ones, like handwoven wool, soft leather lace, and even string. Then we'll continue designing jewelry you could never have dreamed of macramé that you might create. We can create materials in different ways by making one-of-a-kind necklaces, bracelets, earrings, and even jewelry collections and match macramé with a range of other jewelry-making methods, such as wire binding, bead stringing, and even metal clay and leatherwork. We will also be mentioning illustrations in this book to create items such as belts and handbags and even a guitar case, as well as a few wearables, including a halter-top and a light variegated wool scarf. Too cute! Yet that is not the macramé of your mum for this powerful (and fun!) craft. We hope these latest macramé explorations will inspire your own future adventures.

1.1. Materials

The utilitarian origins of Macramé was jute, hemp, and linen, as well as other fabrics that were mainly used for nets and cloth. When sailors and merchants collected various forms of material from the lands to which they sailed, they helped to build the craft — and thus to pass it on. Fast-forward to the present day, where we have new technologies, materials, and, of course, the Internet, and you have the most incredible array of fibers and beads and findings to develop just about anything you can imagine. However, Macramé needs more than just fabric, beads, and finds. Many of the materials that you'll need to build the designs you probably already own in this book. You can easily purchase anything you don't have on hand at your local bead or craft store or, in some cases, even your local hardware store.

1.2. Macramé Boards

Macramé designs need to be fixed on a surface while you work- usually with T pins and/or masking tape. It makes it easy to deal with the cords and helps to keep the ties secure and perfectly arranged. In the nearest bead or art shop, or from online retailers, uniquely made macramé boards are available and operate with most projects. They are usually around 12" / 18" (30 cm / 46 cm) and made of fiberboard. Most macramé boards created have a grid on the surface and rulers along the sides.

They can be removed, but we keep them in place shrink-wrapped or sealed because we consider them very useful guides when we are working. Others also include the simple macramé knots as instructional examples. If your project is too huge to fit on a regular macramé frame, you may need to create your own. Choose a porous surface; you can pin your work easier too. You'll also want to select a surface that you can easily and without damage adhere to, remove, and reposition tape repeatedly. We have used the top of an old desk for larger designs. With a long curtain, we once designed a wooden board of 3' some 6' (91 cm some 183 cm) to get the job done. When you end up building your own macramé surface, then you're going to want to draw a grid on it and add rulers to the edges. When you are working on an unorthodox surface, such as a table or an airplane tray, you may even want to attach a sheet of tape with dimensions written on it so that you have a guide near you.

1.3. Pins and Tape

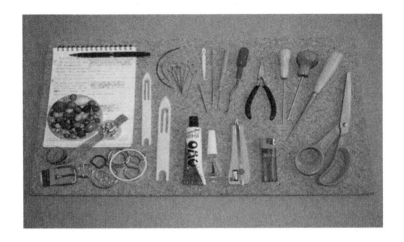

Pins are used for protecting the macramé board project, so it doesn't shift about while you are working. These also come in handy when you integrate different knot sequences and other design features into your designs to keep other strands in place. The most common alternative for macramé is t-pins. These have a good length, and their form makes it convenient for them to attach and uninstall again and again. Ball-end pins used for sewing can also be used, but they are not nearly as robust as T-pins. Avoid push pins and thumbtacks in place, all of which appear to be too low. This also uses masking tape to bind items to the work surface. If you're working on a more delicate surface, it can be a substitute for T-pins, but it's most commonly used to secure "filler cords" — or cords that you tie your working cords around — while tying square and twisting knots. (On the following pages, you'll read more about these.) we like the blue painter's masking tape because it appears to be easier to extract and reposition while you work than standard masking press. Stop removing duct tape, packaging tape, or some other transparent tape; they're all too sticky and can ruin the cords and surface, which are hard to clean all over.

1.4. Scissors, adhesives, wires, cords and beads

Most macramé creations are made of thin fibers, which are easy to cut with a simple pair of art scissors like the ones you probably already own. You might want to get a pair of little trimming scissors designed for sewing to trim the excess length when a project is complete. They'll let you really get close to every knot you want to cut. Any of the projects mentioned in this book use hide and cord suede and leather. We ought to remove a more powerful pair of scissors. From the leather shop, there are beautiful economic scissors which have been our most great all-around scissors. They can handle the hides, yet they are small enough to trim ends near knots, and they're great for just about all the rest. When you're going to deal with these products regularly, buying a higher-quality pair of scissors is worth the cost.

Adhesives

Many of the macramé designs are finished by using adhesive to protect the final knot(s). The type of adhesive that will be used would depend on the materials used. Waxed linen, hemp, cotton, silk, and other fibers are great for white glue. Leather and suede are best suited for rubber cement or contact cement. E-6000 and epoxy are very solid adhesives used to glue non-porous objects together, such as wire and even labradorite beads, which are used for the buckle of the heart belt. All of these adhesives require adequate ventilation during use and should be enforced strictly by all warning labels. Our absolute favourite is The Third, Really strong and flexible, nontoxic, water-based super glue. Bear in mind the toxicity of the glue when deciding which adhesive is best to use for your project, especially if it will come into contact with the skin.

Cords

When you can put a knot into it, you should potentially use it to macramé. Waxed-linen and waxed hemp are two of the most common fiber styles for working with. Both come in a wide range of shades and thicknesses. The wax binding on such strings helps them incredibly good keep a knot. Your knots and knot patterns that arise should be well described. Those cables are sold by beads and jewellery shops, or you can quickly locate them online. Another common macramé material is Rattail, a satin cord that comes in a coloured rainbow and at least three distinct thicknesses. Throughout the 1970s, Rattail became popular but never gone out of style with craftsmen who like to integrate Chinese Knots or Celtic Knots into their work. It can be slippery, so if not secured well knots tied in Rattail can loosen. But the results look so beautiful it really is worth using this material. Another longstanding favourite is polypropylene or polyolefin cord. It is used to make rope for boating, traveling, and any vocation that needs a very sturdy, robust, waterproof material. It's perfect for purses, hammocks, or even the lead and chain idea as well. The selection of colours is not that great, but the utilitarian properties make it a good choice for some projects. It can be sold at the nearest hardware store. Leather and lace suede are great materials made from macramé. There are a variety of lace weights available. Look for the lighter and suppler laces, and skip stiffer ones that may be hard to tie. Consider the shape and function of your project when deciding which type of hiding to use. Is it a jackpot? An asshole? Will the content have to be tough and able to smash, or will it be handled more sensitively? There's a small, lightweight suede I've used for tiny shoes, a beaded curtain, and even a necklace, but we know from experience that a bigger bag will need a thicker and more durable lace. Ultrasound is an alternative to leather and suede. Ultra-suede is a lightweight cloth that avoids stains and has a very similar feeling to suede, which is machine washable. It comes in a wide range of shades and a few different thicknesses. Countless leather, suede, and ultra-suede sizes, designs, and colours are available in your nearest bead, art, or leather shop, as well as online. In several of the accessories in this book, cotton and wool yarns are used, including a scarf, a purse, and even a halter top. There are so many lovely yarns out there, and we must confess that we have always been a bit jealous of knitters and all their choices! We don't want to knead, though. We do want the yarn, though. Experiment with your choices when you are going to the yarn store. You can find varying patterns in a bamboo thread, cashmere, alpaca, angora, and more in addition to can cotton and wool blends. Our favourites are the chunky, variegated yarns (like the one we used with the scarf). Treat yourself to luscious, hand-tinted fibers. The other things to remember when choosing the type of yarn to use: How well does it knot? Unless the material is too slick, then the knot may fall out. Have you got enough material? In the case of certain niche yarns, all they will get can be what they have in stock. We learned this with a purse that we worked on, the hard way. We only bought two cotton skeins while they had three. We used one skein per handle when we attached the yarn to the handles, and noticed that we didn't have enough yarn to complete the job. The last skein has, of course, been sold out. Oops. Oops. We managed to get good, neutral cotton that fit to fill in, but that day we sure learned a lesson. Perhaps it is easier to buy all the particular paint to make sure you have ample products. It's better to have extra than not sufficient.

Wires

The wire is a challenging medium to use for macramé — but if you learn the craft, the effects can be extremely special pieces of jewelry. The essence of metal is not to turn over and over again. It lacks strength, so repetitive bending allows the wire to become brittle so work-hardened. When you bend it back and forth, again and again, it will finally crack. Heavier wire always doesn't want to bend without a huge amount of energy. Most metal macramé is made from thinner diameter wire, which is easier to handle. If it works, it will always stiffen, and the stronger the further you bend it. The wire which is mostly used in this book is silver sterling. When you haven't already dealt with wire, you may want to be more acquainted with it first by using a less costly metal cable. There are several wire types to pick from, including brass, copper, and art wire, which come in a lot of different colours. Some of these tubes, also known as gauges, are available in different thicknesses.

The smaller the number of gauges, the thicker the cable. 20 g-16 g fits well to produce a lock. Because of its thickness, 14 g wire is difficult to bend. We find macramé's best 26 g to 22 g. It is too tough to use a finer gauge, and, in fact, the wire ends up having too many machine marks and kinks. Look for only lighter styles. You'll hear more about the Boho-chic Jewellery Techniques work with metal.

Beads

Without Beads, most macramé projects will not be complete. (We don't think life itself would be complete without beads, but that's just me; in addition to our macramé skills, we also make glass beads.) The available bead options are stunning. When we first learned how to make macramé, there was a limited selection of beads to work with. In general, bead store owners had to travel to get the interesting beads they offered.

The beads that jewellery designers have to choose from today are almost overwhelming, as traders around the world have opened up, as well as technology developments. We use semi-precious gemstones, pearls, antique seed beads, modern seed beads, polished glass lamp work beads, metal beads, bone beads, and even occasionally buttons in this book. We come in different sizes, forms, and hues. One of the most important factors when looking for the beads you'll be using in your project is the size of their holes. Every bead must be able to handle the materials from which you intend to tie. If you can't insert the material into the opening in the ring, you need to widen the opening — probably more effort than you're able to do. You may want to bring a sample of the material you plan to use to the bead store or craft store with you. Alternatively, the wire cover project variant provides a more creative approach to the issue of large bead-small opening. You can use them for the belt buckle in the leather belt project if you find yourself with a bunch of beads that have holes so small they seem totally useless.

1.5. Hardware and findings

Such strictly practical products may not be as enjoyable to pick from, but they're still required. The results for jewelry include clasps and earring wires (unless you want to make your own; see Making Ear Wires). They can be sold in the favorite bead and design shops as well as in other online retailers. Additional hardware can be required for accessories. Belt buckles, chains, and metal rings are excellent options for clothing shops, art and hardware stores, and even accessories stores. Purse covers, from art shops to sewing and clothing outlets, can be obtained from various sites. There are ridged handles (like the pair used in the purse) made of rubber, metal, and bamboo. Leather and leather-like handles offer greater flexibility. And again, you can also find several of those things online.

Tip: We also search the purses and belts for unusual handles and buckles if we're out on our adventures, and we're at a thrift shop. You never know what you might think or what you might be motivated by.

Chapter 2: Tools and Techniques in Macramé

Macramé itself requires little in the sense of tools, but the other methods included in the book do. This chapter states a list of the tools necessary to complete some of the projects. Apart from that, macramé techniques are also compiled here.

2.1. Tools used in Macramé

Jewelry hammer and an anvil or bench block

The two items are used in conjunction with each other; the hammer is used to strike the metal surface, and the anvil or bench block is used to support struck or forged metal. The anvil or bench block is made of steel that is hardened and can withstand the impacts it receives. Round-nose pliers Because of its ability to mold wire into comfortable curves and loops, the jaws are circular and taper to a point, used mainly for jewelry making.

Chain-nose pinchers

These are also used a lot in jewelry, making sometimes called needle-nose pliers to help open jump rings or earring wires or to bend or hold the wire. Wire cutters A hand tool that was used to hack wire ends off.

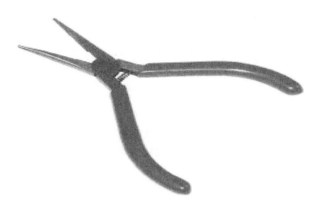

Crimping pliers

A specific type of pliers used in conjunction with crimp beads and the beading wire, which compresses the crimp bead to secure the beading wire and the beads or findings.

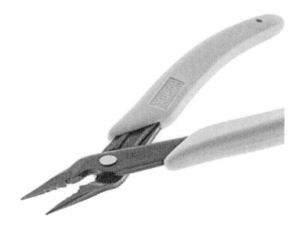

Soft Flex beading wire

A beading wire brand that consists of 49 tiny steel strands

enclosed with a plastic coating. That form of material is often manufactured by many producers and is used to cover it with crimp beads.

Crimp-beads

A type of bead that is used with beading wire to protect the compressed or crimped beads and finds.

Wood dowel

This is a long piece of rounded wood, available in a range of lengths and thicknesses. Dowels have a variety of applications, and it's used to help structure the wire in this situation.

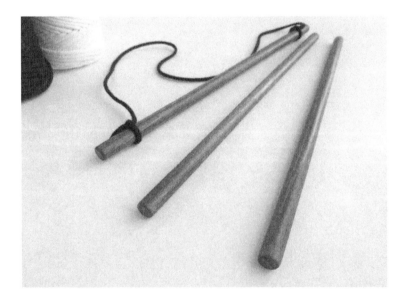

Silver / Black Patina

This patina content, which darkens the silver color, should be handled with great caution using a few acids and nasty chemicals.

Steel wool

The only thing that successfully eliminates the dark patina produced by the silver / black patina solution is a tiny mass composed of thin steel fibers, which is an abrasive material.

Leather hole punch

This leather-working tool has a wheel in varying sizes to cut several types in the hole into leather or suede.

Block and tripod

The tripod provides an elevated surface for soldering the fireproof soldering block and for operating in a safer environment. Butane flares A simple handheld torch that provides enough fire and heat to weld small pieces of silver or fire metal clay.

Butane

The combustible used for butane torches.

Dremel or some other rotary instrument

A multi-tasking tool includes attachments for buffing, polishing, grinding, and drilling, among other items, the materials with which you work. Toaster oven Polymer clay needs baking to cure it, and the toaster oven provides the correct heat for that job. When the toaster oven is filled with polymer clay, it should not be used for cooking. Plastic bobbins These aid with handling extra-long bits of macramé material, making them easy to tie, wrapping and closing the material around the bobbin, encapsulating the material inside, and keeping it stable. The equipment and materials are available from the nearest bead, art, or hardware shops. If you can't find what you need online, search it out. The tool list will allow you to find several of the mentioned products.

2.2. Macramé Techniques

Macramé is a technique of crafting made from a variety of different knots to build patterns and designs. There aren't many knots, but the various differences in the form that they can create are amazing. Many of the knots are used to add a brace to knotting materials; others are used as decorative knots. Throughout this novel, the knots seen in this section are used repeatedly, and you'll continue to use them in all your macramé creations. If you haven't done macramé before, familiarize yourself with them before you launch the projects. Practice the knots in a number of random configurations to see how different kinds of fabrics look and feel.

Overhand Knot

Overhand knots are special knots that can be used to start or finish a piece, or they can be decorative exclusively. Quite a few projects in this book use overhand knots; the yoga mat bag is

even created using an alternating overhand knot pattern.

1. PULL CORDS THROUGH LOOP

To hold it securely, attach the material to be knotted to the top of your macramé board using T-pins. Hold the material in one hand, loosely. Conversely, lay the material over the cord's tail to form a circle.

2. ADJUST KNOT PLACEMENT BEFORE TIGHTENING

Draw the tail and draw taut around the loop, but not too taut. Slide the knot to change its position before completely tightening.

3. TIGHTEN KNOT

Once the knot is in the proper placement, tighten it

4. EXAMINE COMPLETED KNOT

Ascertain, the cords lay properly before moving on to the next

knot.

Lark's Head Knot

The lark's head knot is primarily used as a mounting knot, attaching your material to something else, whether it is another cord or a part of a project, such as a handle, jump ring, or donut bead. It's important to remember that the knot requires twice the length of materials you think you'll need, as you'll be folding it in half, creating two strands. The majority of projects in this book start by tying lark's head knots.

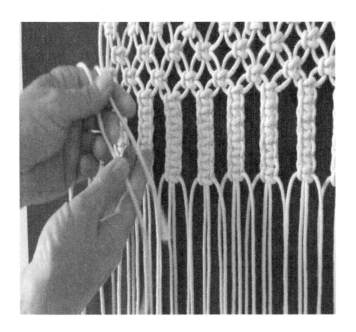

1. PULL CORDS THROUGH LOOP

To keep it firmly, add the material to be knotted to the top of the macramé board using T-pins. Keep the substance in one hand, loosely. Conversely, lay the material over the cord's tail to form a circle.

2. ADJUST KNOT PLACEMENT BEFORE TIGHTENING

Draw the tail and pull taut through the loop, but not too taut. Slide the knot to adjust its position before fully tightening.

3. TIGHTEN KNOT

Once the knot is in the proper placement, tighten it.

4. EXAMINE COMPLETED KNOT

Make sure the cords lay nicely before going onto the next knot.

Half Knot

Among the most common macramé knots are half-knots. They will be bound in two directions: to the left or to the right. In the same direction, repeating half knots form a twist, illustrated on the Square Knot. Illustrated on Square Knot, pairs of alternating half knots create square knots.

1. MOUNT FILLER CORDS

Start the half knot with at least three cords: 2 to tie it and at least one cord to tie it around. (This example uses two fillers. The more filler cords that are used, the thicker the knots will be.) The cords will be numbered from left to right for clarity in the instructions throughout this book. Start by anchoring the 2 and 3 filler cords, by taping them to the macramé board.

2. TIE KNOT

Tied to the left is this half-knot. Cross cords 1 through 2 and 3, making an L. Cross cord

four over 1, then come up under 2 and 3 through the loop that one created. Now cord 4 became cord one, and cord 1 became cord 4. (Simply reverse to tie a half knot to the right)

3. TIGHTEN THE KNOT

Pull 1 and 4 to tighten the knot in any position you wish it to be in. Make sure the filler cords remain taut while the half knot is tightened.

Tip

When the project requires knots for filler cords, such as a square knot or repeated half knot sennit, and those filler cords only have knots wrapped around them, they would need less material than the knotting cords, which do all the job. The filler cords need only be as long as the finished project plus a minimum of 4"–6" (10cm–15 cm) to allow the knot to be tied at the end. And when you weigh the supplies, you only need a bit more than five times overall if you need four times the finished length number for your knotting cords.

Square Knot

The square knot is one of the most popular and versatile knots. It consists of one-half knot tied to the left and one-half knot tied to the right.

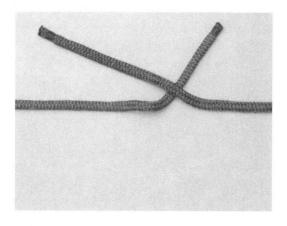

1. TIE AN ALTERNATING HALF KNOT

After setting up the first half tie, on the other hand, you'll undo what you did. Link ties 4 to 2 and 3. Cord 1 lays over 4, then passes below 2 and 3 to come through the formed loop 4.

2. TIGHTEN AND ADJUST

Pull 1 and 4 to hold 2 and 3 toggy, too. And change as needed.

Repeating Half Knot Sennit (also Twisting or Spiral Knots)

1. TIE SERIES OF HALF KNOTS IN ONE DIRECTION

Tie a series a half knots in the same direction (shown here: to the left). You'll start to feel your material wanting to twist.

Occasionally you'll need to un-tape your filler cords and straighten out all of your cords by allowing the twist to occur.

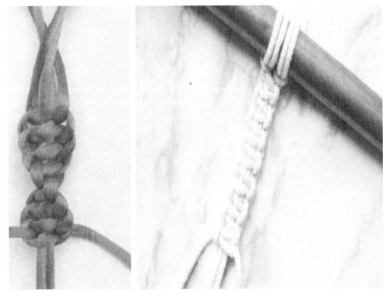

A good solid twist will form after about eight half knots.

Square Knot Sennit

This sennit, or continuous sequence of knots, is simply a repeating series of square knots. Simple straps or other knotted chains that do not twist are often square knot sennits.

1. ALTERNATE TYING LEFT AND RIGHT HALF KNOTS

If the first square knot has been tied, relax it and start tying square knots until you have completed the length you wanted.

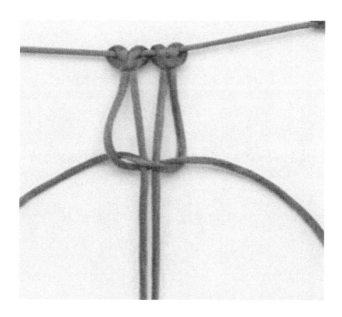

2. CONTINUE TO DESIRED LENGTH

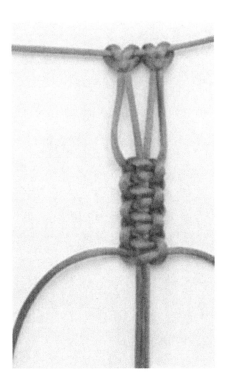

This is a square knot sennit made from 3 full square knots and a half knot. Note that there are 3 loops on the left side of the sennit, and 4 loops on the right. Since these knots were begun on the left side, we will count from the left side in following a trend to keep track of our knot count. Even the loops show you which chord to start next so that you don't miss your position. In this case, if we look at the sennit and see 4 loops on the right side, we know that we have to start the next half-knot on the right. It will complete the fourth square knot, which will also have four loops on the left side until finished.

Square Knot with Alternating Fillers

This knotting sequence is ideal for your macramé project to add beads. The filler cord is switched back and forth, and the resulting pattern allows beads to fit into the gaps. It's a basic but very powerful set, perfect for all jewelry styles, belts and ties.

1. ALTERNATE FILLER CORD FOR EACH SQUARE KNOT

Start on 4 cords. Cover cord 2 with tape and use 1 and 3 cords to form a knot in line. Move the tape to cord 3, and use cords 2 and 4 to tie another square knot. Turn the tape over to cord 2 and tie a separate square knot with cords 1 and 3. Keep on alternating until the target duration is achieved. Notice the holes that form with the 1 and 4 strings, providing ideal spots for attaching beads. This knot sequence is the basis for the button bracelet project on Button and Beads Bracelet.

Alternating Square Knot

The alternating square knot is commonly used to cover decorative patterned areas. It provides a great many style possibilities as a knot pattern. If closely bound, it may create an almost knit-like yarn, often mistaken for knitting or crocheting. If loosely linked, it will have more of a net-like feel to it and can look very lacey. And it can be produced with single square knots or doubles or some singles and some duplicates when creating a pattern.

1. BEGIN FIRST ROW

Cut four lengths of cord about 4' (123cm) long. Tie these on to a mounting cord using lark's head knots. You'll now have eight cords to work with. Number them 1–8. Secure 2 and 3 to the macramé board with tape and tie a square knot with 1 and 4. Remove the tape from 2 and 3, use it to secure 6 and 7, and tie a square knot with 5 and 8.

2. TIE ALTERNATING SECOND ROW

Make sure all the ties are secure and change as needed. Start the next row by securing 4 and 5 cords, and using 3 and 6 cords to tie another square knot. Note the trend is already starting to take form.

3. CONTINUE TO THE DESIRED LENGTH

Repeat step 1 to start the next section. Strengthen and adjust as needed. You should really start looking at a template shape now. Note the flora that developed in the middle of the series of the knot. Go to the length required.

Half Hitch Knot

The half hitch knot, seen below, is the first half of the ever-popular double half hitch knot. The half hitch is most commonly seen vertically on its own, where the full half hitch appears to be used horizontally or diagonally. If a half-hitch knot is repeatedly tied, the resulting sennit would obviously try to curl as the regular half-knot does. Also, the half-hitch is used a lot in a style of macramé called Cavandoli, where the knot is used both vertically and horizontally to construct color patterns. It is sometimes referred to as the Knotted Tapestry or Image Macramé.

1. WRAP KNOTTING CORD AROUND FILLER CORD

Bind a cord length with the head knot of a lark onto a mounting cord, folding the cord in such a way that one side is a third of the length and the other two thirds. To start with, we use 3' (91cm), folded in two strands measuring 1' (30cm) and 2' (61cm), respectively. The knotting cord is the longer strand, the other the filler. Bring the knotting cord over the filler, and then loop and draw firmly under it.

2. REPEAT TO the DESIRED LENGTH

Keep repeating the looping knot sequence over, under, and over until you hit a sennit long enough to curl naturally. The sennit was knotted seven times.

Double Half Hitch Knot

Double half-hitch knots, composed of at least four strings, are used to duplicate sennits to create a seamless visual dividing line as a design feature or, similarly, as a means of joining separate project parts to form a single entity. The knots are wrapped around a filler cord that guides their position, creating elements such as diagonal lines, diamond shapes, or even squiggles.

1. LAY KNOT BEARER OVER WORKING CORDS

Mount up to a mounting cord at least 4–5 cords with the head knots of the lark, making 8–10 working cords. Place a T-pin just below the head-knot of the first lark after cord 1. Place one on the other strings. It is the holder of the chain or filler thread. The other cords around it will then have each knot. The T-pin aids in directing knots.

2. BEGIN TYING A HALF HITCH KNOT

Wrap cord two around the filler with a half-hitch knot that goes over the filler cord and

under and through the created loop.

3. PULL EVERYTHING TAUT

To ensure a well-positioned design feature, pull the first knot close while leaving the filler cord kept taut.

4. COMPLETE DOUBLE HALF HITCH BY REPEATING KNOT

Continue with the same thread, another half hook knot around the filler string.

5. TIGHTEN DOUBLE HALF HITCH

The second knot bolsters the chain and keeps it safely in place. Make sure everything is tight and comfortable, and change as needed.

6. CONTINUE ACROSS ROW OF CORDS

Keep knotting double half hitches from left to right with each chord before the row is completed. Note the coil has grown

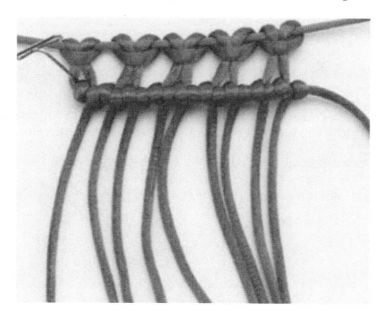

Tip: The amount of extra material you will require for the filler cords that would be used in the double half-hitch knot sequences is something important to remember when you prepare a pattern. When you're not patient, it's easy to run out of rope and you're going to have to splice extra cord into it, which might ruin the design. There will be further conversation with Alternating knotters and Fillers on measuring the sum of materials required for a project on Square Knot Design.

Josephine Knot

It is our favorite of all the macramé knots included. It is a sweet, decorative knot (more for aesthetics than usefulness). It's a little more difficult to execute this knot than the ones

1. LOOP FIRST TWO CORDS

The Josephine knot is better made with over 2 strings. This example uses 4 cords, 2 sets mounted on the head-knots of the lark. Build a loop with cords 1 and 2 which positions the cords above themselves and has the loop aligned to face the board core. The tail ends of the cords face downward toward the macramé board bottom.

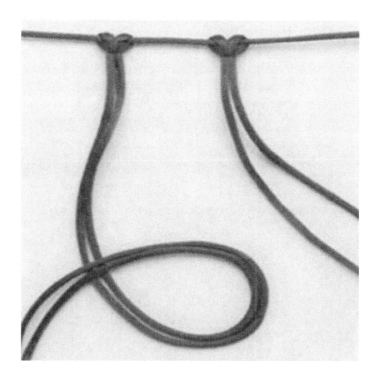

2. PASS REMAINING CORDS UNDER LOOP

Pass both 3 and 4 cords under the 1 and 2 cord loop, and over their tail ends.

3. WRAP CORDS OVER AND UNDER

Move cords 3 and 4 below 1 and 2 over the loop which they created.

4. PASS TAIL THROUGH LOOPS

Move cords 3 and 4 over the top of cords 1 and 2 of the loop, then through the center of the loop below, and out of the cable.

5. BEGIN TO SHAPE KNOT

Tighten the knot carefully, changing cord position and shape.

6. COMPLETE KNOT

The tightened Josephine knot, complete, should take shape as shown.

Square Knot Pattern with Alternating Knotters and Fillers

This square knot variety fits well in series for the development of purse straps and belts. Through moving each alternating knot to the fillers and knotters, you will even out the material use. You can also use this to introduce color play into your macramé in sequence. Just pick various colored knotters and fillers, and tie the knots closely to cover the fillers. If you switch the chord pair positioning, you'll swap colors as well.

1. TIE SQUARE KNOT AND SWITCH CORDS

Mount 2 cables to produce 4 cables on your mounting cord. Secure 2 and 3 cords with tape and tie 1 and 4 square knot. Cut the cover, then use cover to protect 1 then 4.

2. TIE SECOND SQUARE KNOT

Each time tie another square knot with cords 2 and 3 Tighten and change the knot to make sure the cords are smooth and taut.

3. ALTERNATE CORDS AND REPEAT

Replace cords 2 and 3 with 1 and 4 again, then put another square knot together. Note the pattern in the sequence which forms.

2.3. Calculating the amount of material you will need

Macramé allows you to install all your resources before you begin to tie your ties together. This is here where it is really distinct from knitting or crocheting. You use the thread when you go on certain creations, starting from a skein. With macramé, you must first determine the amount of material required and then mount it. It gets really difficult to handle the content. In most situations, including minor ones, you'll need yards or meters of material. At first, it can be a little overwhelming, but with a little practice, you can reliably predict your needs before any project starts. The more complicated your pattern demands the knots, the more material you will need. Unless the concept has lots of places of half or double half hitch knots, you'll have to make up for that, because those knots use a lot of rope. The projects in this book send you material amounts, so if you want to play with combinations or your own macramé designs, you'll need to have a clear idea of how to decide how much material you'll need. Very commonly, you'll need to get each chord at least four to six times what the project's finished duration is. This is a lot of cord or yarn to deal with, which can be a bit of a hassle. The extra-long ends are carefully assembled with different forms of bobbins to facilitate yard management. For Using Bobbins for Thin Cords, two styles of bobbins are featured. Occasionally, if you tie sequences that don't alter the filler strings, as with a basic belt constructed from square knots and/or twist ties, you can save resources. After mounting such strings, the fillers would be only longer than the finished length. Then, the knotting cords should be about four times the final length. There will be a bit of extra content to clip off at the top. Getting extra is always fine, rather than not enough. If, after you complete your project, you find yourself with extra materials, you might want to refer to that in a notebook. Then you can buy a more precise amount if you want to re-create a project later on.

2.4. Using Bobbins for thin cords

When a project requires long lengths of cords, bobbins can make it easier to manage and prevent them from becoming a tangled mess. Any bobbins will work, but the plastic

bobbins shown here are some of the best I've found for working with a thin cord. (If you're using a thick material, like yarn, see the method below, instead.) Bobbins allow you to wrap the material on a spool, then encapsulate the wrapped length inside. These bobbins are available at the local bead or craft retailers or online.

1. WIND CORD AROUND BOBBIN

Wrap the extra cord around the core of the bobbin as if loading a yo-yo.

2. SEAL WOUND CORD INSIDE

Once enough material has been wrapped, close the bobbin to trap the cord and keep it from unrolling.

3. UNWIND MATERIAL AS NEEDED

They're much easier to deal with, with the strings tucked into their bobbins. These bobbins help you to unwind as much as you need to.

Bundling Thicker Fibers

As much as we love the plastic bobbins, you'll need some other way to manage your materials when you're working with thick materials, like yarn or leather lace. That is our favorite form.

1. WIND AND TIE MATERIALS

Move your hand around the circumference of the thread or other dense material. Bind it to a contrasting color with a piece of thread. If more material is needed, simply untie, unwrap and then retie.

Securing a Knot with Glue

With the same step, most macramé projects end: glue and trim. Securing your project's

final knot(s) with a bit of glue before trimming the excess cord length means that wear and tear will not ruin your hard work.

1. GLUE AND TRIM

Apply a small amount of white glue with a T-pin to the inside of the final knot(s) of the project and around it at the start and finish. Squeeze the knot and wash the remaining glue clean. Allow the glue to dry completely before cord end is trimmed as close as possible to the knot.

Chapter 3: Boho-chic patterns for making jewellery and bracelets

While macramé is at the core of all this book's projects, the jewelry projects require a few other basic jewelry-making techniques to complete them. If you're a beginner, don't despair: They're all outlined for you step by step. You'll need to have round-nose pliers, chain-nose pliers, and wire cutters handy (see Tools).

3.1. Wire Wrapping

Wire wrapping is a secure and durable way to create links to add chain, charms, beads, or findings. If you're a beginner, choose an inexpensive, thinner-gauge wire to start (thicker gauges can be difficult to manipulate).

1. WRAP LOOP AROUND PLIERS

Use round-nose pliers to wrap a loop about 1" (3cm) from the end of your length of wire. Use your finger to help guide the tail into place. The rear should be at a 90-degree angle to the fence's body and the loop that was formed. If you want to attach a piece of chain, jump ring, or another link, thread it onto the loop now before wrapping it closed.

2. HOLD LOOP AND WRAP TAIL

Remove the pliers from the inside of the loop and use them to grasp the loop instead. Using chain nose pliers, grasp the wire's tail and wrap it around the body of the wire, just below the loop.

3. FINISH WRAP AND TRIM

Wrap the tail around the wire 2 or 3 times. Trim any excess with wire cutters. Use chain-nose pliers to squeeze the wraps, making sure the end of the wire isn't poking out so it won't scratch the wearer. Add your bead, chain, or finding and wrap another loop flush against it, as in step 1. Again thread on any string, jump rings, or other links desired before wrapping the link closed, as in step 2.

Making Ear Wires

Store-bought ear wires for earrings are available in a variety of shapes, sizes, styles, and types of metal. If you're like me and you prefer to make everything yourself, if possible, you can follow these simple steps to make your own. The only additional tools you'll need are a dowel and maybe a metal file or emery board.

1. WRAP SMALL LOOP WITH PLIERS

Cut two lengths of wire to 2" (5cm) each. Using the round-nose pliers, grasp the end of one wire and make a small loop. Repeat with the other wire.

2. USE DOWEL TO SHAPE

Hold the wire at the loop and gently wrap it around the dowel to shape it. Again, repeat this step with the other piece of wire to ensure the pair of ear wires match.

3. SLIGHTLY BEND EAR WIRES

With round-nose pliers, make a small bend at the top of the ear wire to help it sit in the ear. Remove any sharp edges from the wires with a file or emery board.

Making a Decorative Clasp

Again, you can buy a variety of decorative clasps for your jewelry projects, or you can follow these simple steps to make your own. We designed these years ago and favored them over anything I've seen in a store. These clasps can be made any size you like and from a variety of wire gauges and metal types.

1. HAMMER THE END OF THE WIRE FLAT

Start with a piece of sterling silver 16–18g wire about 2½" (6cm) long. Set it on a bench block and use a jewelry hammer to pound one of the ends of the wire flat.

2. WRAP THE END WITH ROUND-NOSE PLIERS

Use the round-nose pliers to wrap a small decorative loop at the end of the wire. This

small loop is also functional since it gives the hook a smooth end to pass through the other side's loop to connect the necklace.

3. FORM BODY OF CLASP AROUND PLIERS

Still using the round-nose pliers, grip the wire about ¼" (6mm) down from the first small loop and wrap the wire around the thick part of the pliers in the opposite direction of the first loop. Now you have a hook. Adjust the hook as needed with your fingers and the pliers.

4. WRAP LOOP END HOOK OF CLASP

The loop that connects the hook to the rest of the necklace now needs to be formed. Using the round-nose pliers, start a wire wrap loop about ⅛" (3mm) below the bottom of the hook.

5. CLOSE LOOP BY WRAPPING WHILE HOLDING LOOP

Grasp the loop just made with the pliers and wrap the tail of the wire around 2–3 times to form a nice coil.

6. TRIM END CLOSE TO WRAP

Trim any excess wire and smooth the end with a file if it's sharp.

7. HAMMER TO WORK-HARDEN CLASP

Once the shape of the hook is completed, and you're satisfied, hammer the body of the hook lightly on the bench block. This will flatten the hook and, more important, work-harden the metal. "Work-hardening" is a process that strengthens the metal, making it stiffer and less likely to lose its shape.

3.2. Boho-chic pattern Jewellery

Our first real exposure to macramé was at a store called Macraménia, which sold beads of all kinds and other jewelry-making supplies, as well as materials to macramé with. But it was the storeowner's jewelry that left the greatest impression on me. Most of her pieces were created with complex knot sequences in combination with amazing centerpieces and beads. She worked with semiprecious gemstones and beads and what seemed to be the most exotic materials. The pieces were art, one-of-a-kind art to wear. I'm a simple designer, though, with a deep appreciation for fine design and excellent craftsmanship in any piece of jewelry. We like to explore different jewelry-making techniques and have learned quite a few, but we always seem to come back to macramé. It's a craft with admirable simplicity, requiring minimal tools and materials. Most of the designs on the following pages reflect that—, and a few of them were even inspired by our experiences at Macraménia back in the 1970s. This chapter is filled with a selection of jewelry projects that use macramé in ways you may never have expected. We'll explore wire wrapping in versatile ways, showcasing beads in the Wire-Wrapped Necklace and Earrings, letting the wire take center stage in the Turquoise Donut and Wire Bracelet and combining the two in the surprisingly delicate Pearl Chandelier Earrings. We'll move beyond traditional knotting and jewelry techniques when we dabble in mold making and metal clay (and even get to play with fire!) in the Metal Clay Josephine Bracelet. We'll string dainty seed beads to create beaded macramé cord in the Red Seed Bead Spiral Necklace and the Bead Framing Bead Bracelet. And who doesn't like to indulge in a little leather occasionally? The Leather Power Cuff Bracelet is a great project that brings together leather and wire for a big impact. Projects increase in difficulty throughout the chapter, so choose accordingly —but the step-by-step instructions and photos make them all accessible to even beginning crafters. Once you see how fun the techniques are and what a joy the materials are to work with, you'll want to macramé more and more. Pretty soon, you might even be designing your own mod knots.

3.3. Button and Beads Bracelet

The square knot with alternating fillers (see square knot sinnet) used to construct this bracelet is just fabulous. Switching back and forth between filler cords makes a perfect knot sequence for beads: The beads become the focus and the knots just melt back into the scenery. Of course, the button clasp makes a nice design statement, too.

Mod Knots

Overhand knot square knot with alternating fillers (see square knot sennit)

Mod Materials

- Four 2′ (61cm) lengths of 4-ply khaki waxed linen

- One fancy button for the clasp

- 62 extra-small rondelles

- 21 oval, faceted amazonite beads

- macramé board

- T-pins

- masking tape

- craft glue

- scissors

- plastic bobbins

1. TIE THE CORDS TO THE BUTTON

Use an overhand knot to tie the four strands of waxed linen to the back of the button. Glue the knot and let it dry completely. Trim the excess as close to the knot as possible.

2. TAPE BUTTON TO SECURE AND BEGIN KNOTTING

Tape down the button securely. Tie 2 square knots. Thread an oval bead onto cord 4 and thread a rondelle onto cord 3. Tape cord two down to keep it tight and tie a square knot with cords 1 and 3.

3. ADD BEADS WHILE KNOTTING

Remove the tape holding cord two down. Thread an oval bead onto cord one and thread two rondelles onto cord 2. Tape down cord three and tie a square knot with cords 2 and 4. Thread a rondelle onto cord 3.

4. ESTABLISH A PATTERN

Continue threading beads in the same sequence as well as continue switching cords back and forth. Notice the pattern that's forming.

5. COMPLETE CLASP LOOP

Once the desired length for the bracelet is reached, begin stringing the rondelles onto cord 1. This piece will become the loop that passes over the button to close the bracelet. Periodically test the length of the loop by comparing it to the button, and continue stringing until the appropriate length is reached. Tie the loop to the bracelet with strand 4 in an overhand knot. Glue the knot and allow it to dry before cutting the ends close.

3.4. Square Knot Charm Necklace

Here the versatility of the square knot is highlighted by charms added to a simple sennit of square knots. But its simplicity is deceptive. This necklace requires long strands of waxed linen, which will need to be managed properly, or you can end up with a tangled mess of cords. But the results of this necklace are worth the wrangling. Mod Knots overhand knot lark's head knot square knot sennit Mod Materials 4 24' (732cm) strands of

2-ply marine blue waxed linen 1 large Bali silver swirl charm 8 small Bali silver swirl charms 6 small blue glass beads 6 decorative sterling silver headpins 2 decorative fancy hook clasps 1 large jump ring plastic bobbins macramé board T-pins masking tape craft glue scissors round-nose pliers chain-nose pliers wire cutters.

1. PREPARE CHARMS AND KNOT LINEN CORDS TO CENTERPIECE

Create 6 charms by threading a small blue glass bead onto each decorative headpin and using your chain-nose pliers to wire wrap (see Jewelry Techniques) a loop just above each bead to make it into a charm. Set them aside. Hold your 4 lengths of 24' (732cm) waxed linen flush together, fold them in half and mount onto the large Bali silver swirl charm with a lark's head knot. Be careful not to tangle your linen.

2. SECURE CHARM ON BOARD AND BEGIN KNOTTING

Pin this piece to your macramé board with the cords facing you. Wind the ends of the cords in encapsulating plastic bobbins (see Using Bobbins for Thin Cords). Separate the 8 strands into 2 sets of 4 strands — a set for each side of the necklace — and tape down the 2 center strands of each. Begin with the first set of strands and tie 4 complete square knots. Thread a small spiral charm onto cord 4 and tie another square knot.

3. TIE SQUARE KNOT SENNIT AND ADD CHARM

Tie a sennit of 9 square knots. Thread 1 of the charms you created in step 1 onto cord 4. Tie another sennit of 9 square knots.

4. ESTABLISH PATTERN OF SENNITS AND ALTERNATING CHARMS

When the sennit is complete, add a small Bali silver swirl charm to cord 4. Continue repeating the pattern of tying sennits of 9 square knots and adding 1 charm to cord 4, alternating between the 2 types of charms, until 7 charms have been added to that side of the necklace. Then continue tying a sennit of square knots until you reach the desired length of your necklace. Repeat for the other side of the necklace (again starting with a sennit of 4 square knots and small spiral charm for symmetry). Add your charms for this side of the necklace onto cord 1. When the 2 sides are even lengths, tie a hook clasp onto each end with an overhand knot. Coat each knot with a dot of craft glue, let it dry and then trim the ends.

Tip

Having hook clasps on both ends of the necklace makes it easy to add extenders, such as a jump ring or piece of chain, or even to add another necklace so you can wear two strands at once. (We think this would be fabulous paired with the red seed bead necklace.)

3.5. Red Seed Bead Spiral Necklace

As a glass bead maker, we can make ourselves just about any

kind of glass bead we may need or want—except for seed beads. And don't we always want what we can't make? Luckily, you can find seed beads everywhere. So we buy them, always planning to use them later. In designing this necklace, we decided later is now! (Does that make sense? Sure it does.) Go get seed beads you've been squirreling away and make this necklace. It takes the beloved repeated half knot and adds a little sparkle and color to the mix. Each knot has a seed bead on each side. What a pretty necklace this is. And the pattern translates really well for use with other larger beads; just make sure the knotting material is strong enough to handle them.

Mod Knots

Overhand knot repeating half knot sennit (see Square Knot)

Mod Materials

- 2 8' (244cm) lengths of crimson

- 2-ply waxed linen

- 1 2' (61cm) length of crimson

- 2-ply waxed linen

- approximately 500 seed beads in one color

- 2 hook clasps (see Making Ear Wires)

- plastic bobbins

- macramé board

- T-pins

- masking tape

- craft glue

- scissors

1. THREAD SEED BEADS ONTO WAXED LINEN

Begin threading seed beads onto one of the 8' (244cm) strands of waxed linen.

2. COMPLETE FIRST CORD AND FINISH SECOND STRAND

Continue stringing until the length of beaded waxed linen reaches about 2' (61cm) in beaded length, leaving the end on a 6' (183cm) coil. (This is more than is needed, but it's easier to deal with all of the beads now rather than later.) Repeat for a second strand.

3. TIE OVERHAND KNOT AND SECURE STRANDS TO BOARD

Tie the 2 beaded strands and 2' (61cm) strand of waxed linent together in an overhand knot (this knot will be removed later and replaced with a clasp), leaving about 4" (10cm) of extra length at the top to work with at a later time. Allow the beads to naturally slide down to the coil so they're out of your way, as shown. Use a T-pin to pin the knot to a macramé board. The unbeaded strand will be the filler cord; secure it to the board with masking tape. Wind the bottom of each strand around a plastic bobbin to make the strands more manageable to work with. Here we are using plastic bobbins that collapse to hold your working strand in place, as illustrated on Using Bobbins for Thin Cords.

4. TIE HALF KNOT AND ADD FIRST TWO BEADS

Tie a half knot to the left. Slide one bead all the way up each of the left and right strands. Tie another half knot in the same direction and make sure the beads are correctly secured in position.

5. CONTINUE ALTERNATING BEADS AND KNOTS

Slide one more bead up each outer strand. Tie a half knot and again tighten everything into place. Here you can see how the beads are secured into alignment by the knots along the filler strand. 6. KNOT TWISTED, BEADED SENNIT Continue in this way for the length of the entire strand. You'll notice the strand begin to twist as you work. Let it twist, occasionally sliding the knotting strands under the filler and trading sides to allow the twist to naturally form.

7. COMPLETE NECKLACE AND ADD CLASP

Once the beaded sennit has reached the desired length (make sure there is at least 4" [10cm] of tail at the end to work with), detach it from the board. Thread on 1 of the hook clasps and tie an overhand knot to secure it into place. Untie the top overhand knot, thread on the other end of the clasp and secure it with an overhand knot.

8. SECURE KNOT AND TRIM

Secure each of the knots with a dot of craft glue, let it dry and then trim the ends flush with the necklace (securing the knots allows you to cut the ends close).

3.6. Bead Framing Bead Bracelet

Here it is, all glass, all the time. We love tiny beads and am always trying to figure out interesting ways to incorporate them into macramé.

They can be a bit of a struggle to manage, however. This bracelet uses strands of seed beads as the knotting material, and when they're tied, they surround the lamp-work bead strung on the filler, and frame those beads beautifully. The stringing wire is plastic coated steel that is attached to the clasp with crimp beads.

Mod Knots

Square Knot

Mod Materials

- Soft Flex "Soft Touch" beading wire

- 0.019 cut to 3 lengths: 12″ (30cm) for the center strand, and 2 lengths of 2′ (61cm) for the outer strands

- 9 silver crimp beads

- 1 hank of amber seed beads

- 7 handmade lamp-work glass beads, with holes big enough to pass a strand of seed beads through sterling silver triple strand clasp

- macramé board

- T-pins

- crimping pliers

- wire cutters

1. CRIMP WIRE STRANDS TO CLASP

Thread one of the longer pieces of wire with a crimp bead. Pass the wire through one of the loops on the clasp and back through the crimp bead. Pull the crimp bead as close to the loop as possible and use the crimping pliers to secure it in place. Trim the excess wire as close as possible. Attach a strand of wire to each of the other loops in the same way, with the shortest strand in the center.

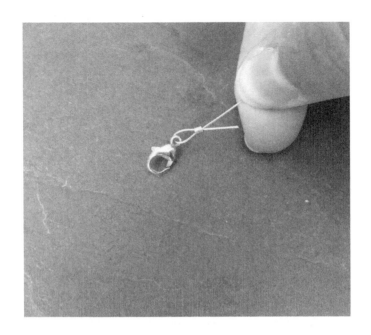

2. STRING SEED BEADS ONTO WIRE

String the seed beads onto the three strands of beading wire. Make sure the beads are strung on tightly, leaving no space or gaps between them.

Add a crimp bead to the end of each strand to hold the beads on, making sure it's tight so the beads don't fall off or loosen while the strands are being knotted.

3. TIE KNOT AND ADD GLASS BEAD

Tie a square knot and then thread a lamp-work glass bead onto the filler strand.

4. CONTINUE TO DESIRED LENGTH AND ADD CLASP

Continue tying knots and adding glass beads until the desired length is reached. Finish with a square knot. Carefully crimp each of the wire ends to the other end of the clasp, as in step 1. Remove excess beads as needed before crimping each wire to the loop. There may be varying amounts of extra beads and wire on each cord, so each one should be handled one at a time, carefully.

5. TRIM EXCESS

Trim the excess beading wire as close to the crimp bead as possible.

Tip:

Soft Flex brand's "Soft Touch" beading wire has amazing flexibility as well as durability. It also doesn't kink as easily as some beading wires do.

3.7. Shibuichi Lentil Necklace

We are blessed to know some incredibly talented bead artists. Many of them are glass bead makers and some are metal smiths. This necklace showcases the work of a couple of these people. The focal bead is made from an alloy of copper and silver, known as shibuichi, which was first formulated in Japan.

The surface color of the bead inspired our color choices for this project as well as the bead and knot combinations.

Mod Knots

Overhand knot repeating half knot sennit (see Square Knot)

72

Mod Materials

- 4 4' (122cm) lengths purple
- 4-ply waxed linen 8 3' (91cm) lengths purple
- 4-ply waxed linen 2 3' (91cm) lengths pink
- 4-ply waxed linen large
- Shibuichi Lentil bead (by Lea Anne Hartman)
- 7 large purple borosilicate beads (by Dan Eister)
- 46 extra-small dichroic beads in purples and pinks
- macramé board
- T-pins
- masking tape
- craft glue
- scissors
- plastic bobbins

1. BEGIN NECKLACE AND ADD FOCAL BEAD

Gather all 14 strands of waxed linen, with their ends lined up evenly, and tie an overhand knot about 6" (15cm) from the end, and slide on the large shibuichi lentil bead, making sure the knot is holding it securely in place.

2. BEGIN HALF KNOT SENNIT

Pin the knot to your macramé board and slide the shibuichi bead snugly up against it. Divide the strands into 2 groups of 7 — each with 2 long purple strands, 4 short purple strands and 1 pink strand — on your macramé board to begin the 2 sides of the necklace. Begin with one side. Arrange the strands so cords 1 and 4 are the longer purple cords, and the pink is cord 7. Wrap the long strands in plastic bobbins. Secure 2 and 3 to the board with tape and tie a sennit of repeating half knots with 1 and 4 until the resulting twist reaches about 2" (5cm) (about 45 knots, 6 full twists).

3. ADD ACCENT BEADS AS YOU WORK

On strands 5, 6 and 7, begin randomly spacing small dichroic beads onto the loose strands, securing each with an overhand knot directly above it and another one below it. Here I'm adding 2 beads to each of 2 loose strands, and 1 to the remaining strand. Keep these beads within the same vertical space as the completed portion of the twist knot.

4. ADD BEAD AND SIMPLIFY CHAIN

Thread on a large borosilicate bead over all 7 strands and slide it so it sits where the knots end; it will naturally rest on the highest small bead below it. Tape 1 of the short purple strands with the other fillers, so now there are 3. Begin tying another series of repeating half knots with 1 and 4, the longer purple cords. Notice that with the new filler, you're absorbing one of the loose strands into the twist knot. Continue the sennit for 2" (5cm).

5. REPEAT TO COMPLETE OTHER SIDE

Repeat steps 3 and 4 until you've reached the desired length and all the loose strands have been absorbed. Tie an overhand knot, thread on a borosilicate bead and secure it in place with an overhand knot. Glue the ends and trim when completely dry. Repeat steps 2–5 for the other side of the necklace. When dividing the strands for this side it's the reverse of the other side. Strand 1 will be the pink strand and the knotting cords will be 4 and 7. At the end, tie an overhand knot. Then, form the excess cord into a loop just big enough to fit over the last borosilicate bead that was tied onto the other side, and tie an overhand knot to complete the clasp. Glue the knots, let dry and trim the ends.

3.8. Quad-Strand Twist Necklace

We think one of the luxuries of macramé is using colorful materials to knot with — especially when working a twist of repeating half knots.

We really enjoy this technique when we can indulge in making something that showcases both color and form, like this quad-strand necklace.

Mod Knots

Overhand knot repeating half knot sennit (see Square Knot)

Mod Materials

- 3 6' (183cm) lengths teal 4-ply waxed linen 3 6' (183cm) lengths turquoise 4-ply

- waxed linen 3 9' (274cm) lengths marine blue 4-ply waxed linen 3 9' (274cm)

- lengths purple 4-ply waxed linen 2 large decorative bead caps or cones (we made

- these out of metal clay, but you can purchase an assortment at your local bead or

- craft store) 1 decorative clasp to coordinate with the cones macramé board

- T-pins

- masking tape

- craft glue

- scissors

- plastic bobbins

1. BEGIN FOUR SEPARATE SOLID-COLORED TWISTING SENNITS

Section your strands of waxed linen by color, hold the ends flush and, 6" (15cm) from the end of each group of cords, tie an overhand knot. Secure each set to the macramé board and wind the strands on plastic bobbins. Begin knotting each trio of strands in sennits of repeating half knots.

2. COMPLETE SENNITS AND REPOSITION STRANDS

Continue until each is the desired length of the focal area, or center, of the necklace (these are about 8" [20cm] long), staggering the lengths very slightly so they don't all end up sitting on top of each other. Remove the overhand knot you've tied at the end of each sennit and line up the unknotted ends. Flip the marine blue sennit around and line up the knots. The longer blue strands will wrap around the others to complete that side of the necklace later. Leave 2 of the purple strands on bobbins and pull them off to the sides. Trim all the other cords to a length of about 5-6" (13–15cm).

3. TIE PURPLE STRANDS AROUND OTHERS

Begin tying the purple strands around all the center strands in a sennit of repeating left half knots. Notice the thickness of the twist that forms. This will serve as one side of the necklace surrounding the focal section you created in steps 1–2. Continue until this half of the necklace has reached the desired length.

4. SLIDE ON DECORATIVE CONE

Remove the piece from your macramé board. Slide a decorative bead cap down to where all the strands connect to hide that spot.

5. FINISH OTHER SIDE AND ADD CLASP

Start on the other side of the necklace by gathering the unknotted sections, laying them together, positioning the marine blue strands off to either side, and securing all the others with tape. Trim the filler cords to a length of 5–6" (13–15cm). Repeat steps 3–4 using the blue strands to tie a repeating half knot sennit around the others until the length is even with the other side. Tie each group of strands to the clasp with an overhand knot. Glue the knots, let them dry and trim the ends.

3.9. Swallow Necklace And Earrings Set

So we have become addicted to the online craft marketplace www.etsy.com, both as a seller and as a buyer. That's where we found these small swallow charms — they're all over etsy.com, showcased in really lovely pieces of jewelry.

This project uses a nice variety of knots and a sprinkling of tiny seed beads to accent the little birds.

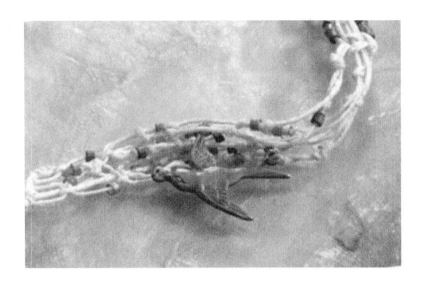

Mod Knots

Necklace

Overhand knot, lark's head knot repeating half knot sennit (see Square Knot) alternating square knot double half hitch knot.

Earrings

Half hitch knot

Mod Materials

Necklace

- 8 8' (244cm) lengths ivory 2-ply waxed linen

- large antique brass swallow charm

- 4 small antique brass swallow charms

- antique brass hook clasp
- an assortment of seed beads (Aiko) in Satin Sea Serpent Green AB, Matte Raku
- Teal/Blue Iris and Matte Raku Steel Blue
- macramé board
- T-pins
- masking tape
- craft glue
- scissors

Earrings

- 2 2' (61cm) lengths ivory 2-ply waxed linen
- 2 ½" (1cm) diameter jump rings
- 2 small antique brass swallow charms
- 18 seed beads (Aiko) in an assortment of Satin Sea Serpent Green AB, Matte
- Raku Teal/Blue Iris and Matte Raku Steel Blue
- 2 oversized antique brass ear wires
- craft glue
- scissors

Necklace

1. BEGIN NECKLACE

One at a time, tie 4 strands of the ivory waxed linen onto each side of the swallow centerpiece with lark's head knots, which gives you 8 strands on each side. Pin the centerpiece to the macramé board. Start on the right side of the necklace, tie an overhand knot with strand 8 and thread on a teal/blue seed bead. Secure the bead in place with another overhand knot.

2. CREATE DIAGONAL SERIES OF DOUBLE HALF HITCH KNOTS

Lay strand 1 at a slight diagonal across strands 2–8. This will be the knot bearer for a line of double half hitch knots. One at a time, knot each of the 7 strands to strand 1 using a double half hitch. Strand 1 now becomes strand 8. Thread 1 seed bead onto each of strands 1, 3, 5 and 7 in this color order: green, steel blue, teal/blue, green. Lay strand 1 at a slight diagonal across strands 2–8. Again knot each of the 7 strands to strand 1 using a double half hitch. Strand 1 now becomes strand 8.

3. CONTINUE DIAGONAL DESIGN ELEMENTS

Tie an overhand knot on strand 1, thread on a steel blue bead, and secure it with an overhand knot. Lay 8 across strands 1–7 at a diagonal and one at a time, starting with strand 7, knot each of the strands to the knot bearer with a double half hitch. Strand 8 is now 1. Begin the first row of the alternating square knot pattern: Tie a square knot with strands 1 and 4 around fillers 2 and 3. String a teal/blue seed bead onto 1 and a steel blue seed bead onto 4. Tie a square knot with 5 and 8 around fillers 6 and 7. String a green seed bead onto 5 and a steel blue seed bead onto 8.

4. CONTINUE KNOTTING AND ADD SWALLOW CHARM

Continue with 2 more rows of alternating square knots, without adding any seed beads in these rows. With strand 8, leave a little bit of space, tie an overhand knot, slide on the small swallow charm and tie another overhand knot. Make sure to use a swallow that will be flying toward the inside of the necklace.

5. THREAD ON SEED BEADS AND TIE OVERHAND KNOTS

Among strands 1–7, randomly secure seed beads in assorted colors with pairs of overhand knots for a vertical space of about ½" (1cm). Then, tie together pairs of strands—1 and 2, 3 and 4, 5 and 6, and 7 and 8—each with an overhand knot forming a diagonal line, as shown.

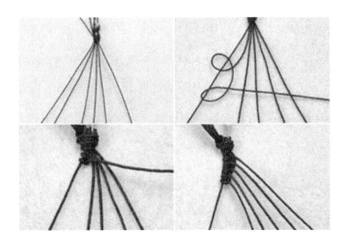

6. ESTABLISH PATTERN OF SQUARE KNOTS AND SEED BEADS

Take strands 1 and 2 in one hand and 7 and 8 in the other and tie them in a double-thickness square knot around 3–6. Thread 3 assorted seed beads onto strand 1 and 3 seed beads onto strand 8. Repeat the double-thickness square knot. Thread 3 assorted seed beads onto strand 1 and 3 seed beads onto strand 8. Repeat the double-thickness square knot. Again thread 3 assorted seed beads onto strand 1 and 3 seed beads onto strand 8. Repeat the double-thickness square knot.

7. ADD SWALLOW CHARM AND TIE DOUBLE HALF HITCH KNOT

Thread the swallow charm onto strands 1 (the tail end) and 8 (the nose end), sliding it down to rest on top of strands 2–7, securing it with an overhand knot on each strand. This time the

84

swallow should face the opposite direction from the first swallow. Thread 5 seed beads onto strand 1, lay it diagonally over the other strands, and tie them each, one at a time, to this strand with a double half hitch knot. Strand 1 now becomes strand 8.

8. TIE TWISTING SENNIT OF REPEATING HALF KNOTS

Leave about ½" (1cm) of vertical space and then begin tying a sennit of repeating half knots in a twist, using strands 1 and 8 to tie around fillers 2–7. Continue the nice, thick twist for about 1" (3cm).

• TIE EVENLY SPACED SQUARE KNOTS

Tie four square knots with strands 1 and 8 around fillers 2–7 in ½" (1cm) increments.

9. COMPLETE NECKLACE IN MIRROR IMAGE

Repeat on the other side, executing steps 1–8 in the reverse direction to create the mirror image of one side on the other side. Finish by tying one half of the clasp to each end of the necklace with an overhand knot. Coat these knots with craft glue, let them dry completely and trim the ends.

Earrings

11. KNOT THREAD TO RING AND BEGIN MACRAMÉ

Tie one of the 2' (61cm) strands of waxed linen onto one of the

½" (1cm) diameter jump rings, leaving a trail of about 1½" (4cm). Working counterclockwise, tie 4 half hitch knots and thread a seed bead onto the strand tight against the ring.

12. REPEAT PATTERN TO COMPLETE HOOP

Repeat in this pattern: 4 half hitch knots, seed bead, 4 half hitch knots, nose end of swallow charm, 4 half hitch knots, seed bead, 4 half hitch knots, seed bead, 4 half hitch knots, tail end of swallow charm. Then alternate 4 half hitch knots with seed beads until the entire hoop is covered. Use the working strand and the tail of the first knot to tie the ear wire onto the earring. Coat the knot with glue, let it dry and trim the ends close.

Tip

Tying half hitch knots is a great way to cover a jump rings as in this project as well as the belt project. Half hitch works with all types of materials and can be used to cover just about anything. You can cover up something not so attractive or create your own shapes with wire that can then be covered with leather, linen or whatever suits your project. Half hitch knots do naturally twist as you know them so you must constantly adjust the knots to prevent it from happening.

3.10. Wire-Wrapped Necklace And Earrings

The rock quartz beads in this project spoke to us when we

bought them. They basically said, "Buy me!" but we weren't quite sure what we would end up using them in. When the beads found themselves nestled among some amazonite beads in our stash, that's when we knew we had to macramé these beads with wire.

Of course, a necklace would need earrings to complete the pretty set. You will need your fancy handmade clasp and ear wires and wire wrapping skills for this project.

Mod Knots

Necklace

Square Knot wire wrapping (see Jewelry Techniques)

Earrings

Square Knot

Mod Materials

- Necklace 9 8" (20cm) lengths

- 22-gauge sterling silver wire 4 2" (5cm) lengths

- 20-gauge sterling silver wire

- 2 4" (10cm) lengths medium weight sterling silver chain

- 4 rock quartz oval beads

- 7 medium amazonite rondelles

- 10 tiny amazonite rondelles

- 2 round swirl bone beads

- 2 extra small round bone beads fancy hook clasp (see Making Ear Wires)

- macramé board

- T-pins

- masking tape

- round-nose pliers

- chain-nose pliers

- metal file

- wire cutters

Earrings

6 6" (15cm) lengths

22-gauge sterling silver wire

2 sterling silver ball ended headpins

4 rock quartz oval beads

2 medium amazonite rondelles

4 tiny amazonite beads

2 extra small round bone beads pair of fancy handmade ear wires (see Making Ear Wires) round-nose pliers chain-nose pliers wire cutters

Necklace

1. CREATE WIRE WRAPPED LOOP TO START THE NECKLACE

Start with the center section of the necklace: Take 3 8" (20cm) lengths of 22-gauge sterling silver wire, hold them together tightly and wire wrap a closed loop. Trim any excess wire and file any sharp ends.

2. SECURE TO BOARD AND ADD BEADS

Pin the wire to the board through the loop. Make sure it's nice and secure. Thread on an extra small bone bead, an amazonite rondelle and a rock quartz bead to the filler wire, then secure it to the board with tape.

3. TIE WIRE KNOT AND TIGHTEN WITH PLIERS

Begin a square knot by tying a half knot. Grasp each knotting wire with a pair of pliers and pull gently but firmly to tighten the knot, being very careful not to leave marks on the wire. See how the wire nicely frames the beads.

4. COMPLETE FIRST SQUARE KNOT

Finish the other half of the square knot and again pull with pliers to tighten the knot.

5. CONTINUE ADDING BEADS AND KNOTTING

Thread onto the filler wire another amazonite bead and then tie another square knot, always using pliers to aid you with the wire. Add another quartz, an amazonite and the other bone bead. Remove the section from the board and wrap a loop with the remaining wire.

6. WIRE WRAP LOOP TO FINISH NECKLACE SEGMENT

Complete the loop by grasping it carefully with the round-nose pliers and wrapping the tail around a couple of times. Trim any excess wire and adjust the loop. Make sure all 3 strands of wire are flat and the loop looks attractive. There should be no exposed sharp points on the wire ends. File the ends if necessary to smooth them. This piece will serve as the center segment of your necklace.

7. START NEW SEGMENT CONNECTED TO CENTERPIECE

Begin your next section with a loop made from another 3 8" (20cm) strands of 22-gauge wire. Thread the loop onto the completed section and then wire wrap that loop closed. Trim any excess wire and file any sharp ends.

8. BEGIN BEADING AND KNOTTING PATTERN

Pin the necklace parts to the board at the new loop as shown. Thread a tiny amazonite bead onto the filler wire, tape that wire down and tie a square knot with the others. Carefully use your pliers to pull the knot tight.

9. COMPLETE THIS SECTION AND REPEAT ON OTHER SIDE

Follow this sequence: quartz bead, square knot, tiny amazonite bead, swirl bone bead, tiny bead, and square knot. Add a medium amazonite rondelle onto the filler wire (removing the tape to thread it on, then replacing the tape) and tie a square knot. Add a tiny amazonite bead and wire wrap a closed loop.

Trim the excess wires and smooth the ends. Repeat steps 8 and 9 for the other side of the necklace.

10. WRAP A LOOP TO CONNECT THE PARTS

Using one of the shorter lengths of 20-gauge silver wire, wrap a loop and thread it onto the loop at either end of the necklace. This will help attach chain to the back of the necklace. Close the loop.

11. ADD CHAIN TO NEW LINK

Add an amazonite bead and wrap a loop. Thread a piece of chain onto the loop and then wrap the loop shut.

12. ATTACH CLASP WITH LINK

At the end of the length of chain, repeat the wire wrap link this time using a tiny amazonite bead. Wrap the final loop and thread on the clasp. Close the loop.

13 ADD CHAIN AND FINISH NECKLACE

Repeat the steps to attach the chain and clasp to the other side of the necklace. When the final loop is wrapped, make it a bit larger and close it. The hook will attach here.

Earrings

14. CREATE BEAD DANGLE

The earrings are made up of two sections. The top section is like a section of the necklace. The other section is a dangle made with a headpin. Start the macramé section by wire wrapping a loop with the 3 strands of wire to a jump ring. Pin the ring and wires to the macramé board and thread a bone bead, then an amazonite rondelle onto the filler wire. Tape the filler down and tie a square knot around it. Add a quartz bead to the filler and tie another square knot around it. Add a tiny amazonite bead and finish this section with a closed wire wrapped loop.

Thread a quartz bead and an amazonite bead onto a sterling

silver headpin. Make a loop and thread the headpin onto the loop of the top section of the earring and then close the loop. Trim any excess wire. Repeat for the other earring.

15. ATTACH EAR WIRES

When the earrings are complete, attach them to ear wires — either those you've made yourself (see Making Ear Wires), as shown here, or store-bought findings — by opening up the loop on the ear wire and slipping the jump ring into it. Make sure the earring is facing the correct direction. Close the loop on the ear wire. Repeat with the other earring.

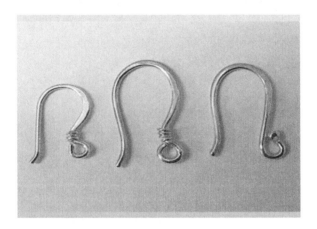

Variation: Chunky Amethyst with Suede

The variation of this necklace employs the same knots, just different materials. What's different about this necklace is the use of suede and waxed linen with chunky beads. The amethyst beads had holes that could not accommodate the suede, but we really wanted to find a way to combine the two in a project. By using waxed linen to string through the beads, we found we could make it work. The suede and linen were first tied to a wire-wrapped loop, and that loop was later connected to the chain. The beads were strung onto the linen and the suede tied around the beads. Large silver caps were used to camouflage the connection. This necklace is finished the same way as the quartz and amazonite necklace.

3.11. Turquoise Donut And Wire Bracelet

Donut beads are used in macramé all the time. They're perfect for having materials mounted with a lark's head knot to them.

Donuts are available in many types of materials and sizes, but we like turquoise the best. This bracelet combines small donuts with wire macramé and some really interesting glass beads, and the results are so cool.

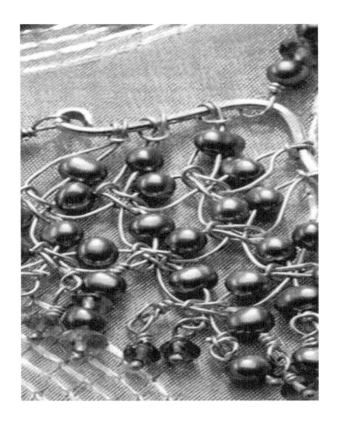

Mod Knots

Lark's head knot Square Knot repeating half knot sennit (see Square Knot) alternating square knot

Mod Materials

- 6 14" (36cm) lengths

- 26-gauge sterling silver wire

- 10 24" (61cm) lengths

- 26-gauge sterling silver wire

- 2 small turquoise donut beads

- 2 small barrel raku glass beads

- 3 extra small raku glass beads

- 1 extra small turquoise nugget

- 4 large jump rings or chain links

- 1 lobster claw clasp

- macramé board

- T-pins

- masking tape

- round-nose pliers

- chain-nose pliers

- wire cutters

- metal file

1. ATTACH WIRE TO DONUT BEAD

Use lark's head knots to mount 2 pieces of the shorter silver wire to a turquoise donut bead. Pull the wires tight with chain-nose pliers.

2. SECURE TO BOARD AND TIE KNOT

Attach the donut to the macramé board with a T-pin and tape down 2 filler wires. Tie a square knot with 1 and 4 using the pliers to gently pull the knot tight.

3. ADD GLASS BEAD AND CLASP

Thread a glass bead onto all 4 wires, and wrap a loop. Thread a lobster claw clasp onto the loop and wrap the loop closed. Trim any excess wire and file any sharp ends.

4. KNOT TWISTING SENNIT ON SECOND DONUT BEAD

Use lark's head knots to mount 2 of the longer pieces of silver wire to the other turquoise donut bead. Secure the donut bead to the macramé board with T-pins and tie a sennit of 10 repeated half knots.

5. ATTACH SECTIONS WITH WIRE-WRAPPED LOOP

Use the round-nose pliers to wrap a rather large loop with the wires and thread on the

other turquoise donut. Make sure there's enough room in the loop to accommodate the size of the donut. Wrap the loop closed and trim away excess wire.

6. MOUNT NEW SECTION TO OPPOSITE SIDE OF DONUT

Use lark's head knots to mount 2 pieces of the shorter wire to the turquoise donut that the twisting knot is on. Pin the piece to the board and tie a square knot. Remove the piece from the board and thread a glass bead onto all 4 wires. Wrap a loop with the wires and thread a jump ring onto the loop. Close the loop with a couple of wire wraps. Trim any excess wire and file any sharp ends.

7. CREATE ALTERNATING SQUARE KNOT SECTION

To start the next section, take 4 strands of the longer pieces of wire and mount them onto a jump ring with lark's head knots. Secure the jump ring to the board with T-pins. Divide the 8 wire strands into 2 sections of 4. Tape down wires 2 and 3 and 6 and 7 and tie 2 square knots, side by side, with 1 and 4 and 5 and 8, respectively. Remove the tape. Now secure wires 4 and 5 and tie a square knot with wires 3 and 6 to form a second row. Repeat rows 1 and 2 to form an alternating square knot sequence. Remove the wires from the board, thread a small glass bead onto all 8 strands and wrap a loop. Thread the jump ring from the last step onto the loop and wrap it closed, trimming any excess wire.

8. REPEAT ALTERNATING SQUARE KNOT SEQUENCE

Repeat step 7 on the other side of the same jump ring. When the small bead is threaded

onto the wires, wrap a loop and add a jump ring to the loop. Wrap the loop closed and trim any excess wire.

9. COMPLETE BRACELET

The last section of this bracelet uses 2 of the shorter pieces of wire connected to the last jump ring with a lark's head knot. Tie a half knot to start a square knot. Thread the small turquoise bead and a small glass bead onto the filler wires. Complete the square knot. Wire wrap a loop and thread on the last jump ring. This is what the lobster claw clasp attaches to close the bracelet. Close the loop and trim any excess wire.

3.12. Pearl Chandelier Earrings

The macramé almost disappears in these chandelier earrings. As the wire creates a lace-like effect that frames the beads perfectly, the design becomes all about the bead choices. In this case, we have opted for pearls and iolite, but this project works well with many varieties of pearls and semiprecious beads (you might try mixing up your choice of wire, too!).

Dangles add movement and fluidity. Mod Knots lark's head knot alternating square knot Mod Materials 2 2¼" (6cm) lengths 16-gauge sterling silver wire 12 12" (30cm) lengths 26- gauge sterling silver wire 2 2" (5cm) lengths 22-gauge sterling silver wire 30 26- gauge sterling silver headpins 54 small freshwater pearls 24 extra small faceted iolite beads pair of fancy hand-made ear wires (see Making Ear Wires) macramé board T-pins masking tape round-nose pliers chain-nose pliers wire cutters hammer bench block or anvil.

1. FORM TWO IDENTICAL EARRING FRAMES

Take both lengths of 2¼" (6cm) 16-gauge wire and hammer the tip of each end flat. Use your fingers to bend one of the pieces slightly in the middle, and then use round-nose pliers to roll up each of its flattened ends into curls. Repeat with the other piece of wire to create an identical frame to ensure the earrings match.

2. MOUNT WIRES TO FRAME

Pin one of the wire frames to the macramé board. Take 6 of the 12" (30cm) lengths of 26-gauge wire and attach each one to the frame, one at a time, with lark's head knots. Pull each knot tight with chain-nose pliers. You should now have 12 wire strands, 6 on each side of the wire frame.

3. ADD PEARLS AND BEGIN KNOTTING

Position wires 1–4 and 8–12 out of the way, as shown, so you can first work with the others. String 1 pearl onto wire 6 and 1 onto wire 7. Tie strands 5 and 8 in a square knot around these fillers, tightening the knots by pulling gently but firmly with pliers.

4. ESTABLISH ALTERNATING SQUARE KNOT PATTERN

Begin the alternating square knot pattern by positioning wires 3–4 and 8–9 back in your work area. Thread a pearl each onto wires 4, 5, 8 and 9. Tie 3 and 6 in a square knot around 4 and 5, and tie 7 and 10 in a square knot around 8 and 9.

5. WIRE WRAP ENDS INTO LOOPS

Continue tying the alternating square knot pattern until 4 rows have been established. Then, on each of strands 1–3 and 10–12, thread on a freshwater pearl, wire wrap the strand into a small closed loop beneath the pearl and trim any excess wire. For all of the other strands, finish with a small closed wire-wrapped loop.

6. ADD IOLITE DANGLES

Thread an iolite bead onto a headpin. Twist the pin into a loop just above the bead. Thread this into the loop at the bottom of strand 1 and wire wrap it closed to complete the dangle design element. Repeat to add dangles in this order, from left to right: freshwater pearl, iolite, freshwater pearl, iolite, iolite, stack of 4 alternating iolites and freshwater pearls as a center dangle, and then the right side of the earring mirroring the left (iolite, iolite, freshwater pearl, iolite, freshwater pearl, iolite

7. ADD LINK TO CONNECT EAR WIRE

Add a dangle to each spiral end of the frame created in step 1 by threading first a freshwater pearl and then an iolite bead onto a headpin, twisting the pin into a loop just above the beads and threading the loop through the end of each spiral before securing it with a wire wrap. Finish the earring by cutting a

short length of wire, making a wire-wrapped loop at one end, threading on a freshwater pearl, iolite bead and freshwater pearl in that order, and then finishing with a wire-wrapped loop that is threaded through the top of the frame of the earring.

Add the ear wire by slightly opening the loop of the ear wire, threading the earring onto it, and closing the ear wire loop. Repeat the process beginning with step 2 to create a second earring, being sure to check your work periodically against the first earring to be sure the two match.

3.13. Leather Power Cuff Bracelet

This cuff bracelet is fierce! You almost have to make two so you can have twice the power.

It's a variation of a cuff bracelet we designed awhile back for some fashion industry clients. The original cuff was made out of satin rattail, but in modifying our own version, we wanted it in leather. Who wouldn't? So, we incorporated heavyweight

silver wire for structure and two extremely cool silver wire coil buttons to secure the cuff.

Mod Knots

Lark's head knot double half hitch knot

Mod Materials

- 2 8" (20cm) lengths
- 12-gauge sterling silver wire 1 16"
- (41cm) length 16-gauge sterling silver wire
- 1 20" (51cm) length 16-gauge sterling silver wire
- 2 10' (305cm) lengths black leather lace
- 1 12' (366cm) length black leather lace
- 10 8' (244cm) lengths black leather lace
- macramé board
- T-pins
- masking tape
- leather contact cement
- scissors
- round-nose pliers
- chain-nose pliers

- wire cutters

- jewelry

- hammer bench block or anvil

- measuring tape

- paper pencil jeweler's saw

1. CREATE CUFF TEMPLATE

You'll need 2 measurements: The circumference of the wrist of the intended recipient (at the bottom of the wrist where the cuff will rest) and the circumference of the forearm about 7" (18cm) up from the wrist. Transfer those 2 measurements to a piece of paper by drawing 2 centered parallel lines of those lengths 7" (18cm) apart. Connect the lines and then cut the template out. Wrap it around the wrist to test the fit and adjust as necessary.

2. ADD LEATHER STRIPS TO HEAVY WIRE

Tie a short length of leather lace to each of the 8" (20cm) lengths of heavy 12-gauge sterling silver wire. (Note: When first cutting the wire to size, you'll need a jeweler's saw, rather than ordinary wire cutters, to cut such thick wire.) Secure the knots and some of the leather onto the wire with leather contact cement, allow to the cement to dry and trim the ends.

3. MOUNT CUFF TEMPLATE TO BOARD AND LEATHER TO WIRE

Tape your cuff template to your macramé board with the longest edge on the left and one of the diagonals at the top, being careful not to completely conceal the edges of your pattern (you'll need to see them). Tape one of the leather-covered wire pieces from step 2 along the top edge of your pattern. Secure one of the 10' (305cm) pieces of black leather lace to the furthest left position on the top bar with a lark's head knot. Then secure each of the 10 8' (244cm) pieces of lace side by side with lark's head knots across the rest of the bar.

4. BEGIN KNOTTING DIAGONAL DESIGN ELEMENTS

Lay strand 1 across strands 2–22 at a very slight diagonal and secure each strand to it with a double half hitch knot. Strand 1 now becomes strand 22. Again, lay strand 1 (formerly strand 2) across strands 2–22 at a parallel diagonal and secure each strand to it with a double half hitch knot. Again strand 1 becomes strand 22.

5. CONTINUE DOUBLE HALF HITCH KNOTS

Lay strand 22 across strands 1–21 at a slight diagonal (a bit less slight than in the previous step), hold it in place with a T-pin at the edge to help direct the angle, and secure each strand to it with a double half hitch knot, working right to left. Strand 22 now becomes strand 1. Again, lay strand 22 (formerly strand 21) across strands 1–21 at a parallel diagonal and secure each strand to it with a double half hitch knot.

6. SECURE ENDS TO SECOND WIRE

Repeat step 4. Repeat step 5. Repeat step 4. Lay the other piece of leather covered wire from step 2 across the bottom edge of the pattern and secure each strand to it with a double half hitch knot. Coat all of the knots with leather contact cement, let them dry and trim the ends. 7. HAMMER WIRE FLAT Take a 16" (41cm) piece of 16-gauge silver-colored wire and twist it into a small loop in the center and hammer it flat and closed.

8. FORM SPIRAL CLOSURE WITH PLIERS

Wind one end of the wire into a spiral, working toward the center of the piece. Working in the opposite direction, wind the other end of the wire into another spiral. Make sure the size is right to fit through the spaces between the rows of knots on the cuff. Hammer the spirals flat to work harden them.

9. CREATE LARGER SPIRAL CLOSURES

Repeat steps 7 and 8 to make another coil button for the cuff, this time beginning with a 20" (51cm) piece of wire to make slightly larger spirals. Use small scraps of leather lace to tie one of these buttons onto each end of one of the leather-covered wires about 1" (3cm) in from the end.

10. ADJUST FIT AS NECESSARY

Push the ends of the spirals through the slots in the other end of the cuff bracelet to make sure they'll secure it closed. Adjust their positioning if necessary.

3.14. Inspired Asymmetry Necklace

Collecting beads has been a passion of mine since childhood. Our bead collection has grown so much through the years that sometimes it's like having our very own bead store. Couple that with all of the jewelry-making techniques we have learned along the way, and we believe this necklace is the perfect example of the two passions meeting and greeting. It combines wirework, a diverse array of macramé knots and labradorite beads in different shapes and sizes. Check out the centerpiece! What a bead!

Mod Knots

Overhand knot lark's head knot repeating half knot sennit (see Square Knot) alternating square knot double half hitch knot half hitch knot

Mod Materials

- 3 8' (244cm) lengths khaki

- 4-ply waxed linen 3 8' (244cm) lengths

- turquoise 4-ply waxed linen 1 10' (305cm) length khaki

- 4-ply waxed linen 1 10' (305cm) length

- turquoise 4-ply waxed linen

- 1 12" (30cm) length khaki

- 4-ply waxed linen 1 12" (30cm) length turquoise

- 4-ply waxed linen 2' (61cm)

- 26-gauge sterling silver wire

- 7 26-gauge sterling silver ball headpins

Extra-

- large faceted labradorite bead

- large clear carved crystal flower

- One medium faceted labradorite bead

- 19 small aqua transparent glass beads

- Seven small labradorite beads in various shapes

- 1 aqua glass button

- 16-gauge sterling silver wire oval or wire shaped into a ring and soldered closed and hammered, about 2" × 3" (5cm × 8cm)

- macramé board

- T-pins

- masking tape

- craft glue

- scissors

- round-nose pliers

- chain-nose pliers

- wire cutters

1. THREAD LINEN THROUGH BEAD AND SECURE KNOT

Use the 2 shortest lengths of waxed linen to thread through the extra-large labradorite bead that will serve as the centerpiece of the necklace. Knot the cords tightly with an overhand knot as shown, forming a close-fitting loop around the bead, and glue the knot. When the glue is completely dry, trim the ends.

2. ATTACH THREAD FOR BOTH SIDES OF THE NECKLACE

Tape the extra-large labradorite bead to your macramé board, with the loop facing toward you. At the right side of the loop, working left to right, attach 3 8' (244cm) khaki strands, then 3 8' (244cm) turquoise strands, one at a time onto the loop, lining the knots up side by side. Working right to left using lark's head knots, attach the 10' (305cm) pieces of each color of waxed linen side by side onto the left side of the loop as shown.

3. TIE SENNIT AND ATTACH FLOWER BEAD AND GLASS BEAD

Use the four strands at the left of the loop to tie a sennit of repeating half knots to form a twist that's about ¾" (2cm) long (about 20 knots). Take strands 2 and 3, thread them through the hole in the center of the flower bead (from the wrong side through to the front) and thread on a small light blue glass bead. Thread them back through the center of the flower — the small bead will act as a stopper, and this will serve to thread the flower onto the necklace.

4. CREATE SENNIT AND ADD LABRADORITE BEAD

Begin another series of repeated half knots to form a twist that's about 1" (3cm) long. Thread cords 2 and 3 through the medium-sized labradorite bead, rejoin them with the other two cords on the other side of the bead, and begin tying another series of repeated half knots. Make sure the bead sits snuggly within the twisting sennits.

5. CONTINUE SENNIT AND CREATE CLASP

Continue until this side of the necklace has reached your desired length. Combine strands 1 and 2 and thread about nine

small blue-tinted glass beads onto them, or until you've formed half a loop that's an appropriate size to slide over the glass button that will serve as the other half of your clasp. Thread the other nine small aqua transparent glass beads onto strands 3 and 4. Tie all the strands together into a loop with an overhand knot. Coat the knot with a dot of craft glue, let it dry, and trim the ends.

6. CREATE DIAGONAL DESIGN ELEMENTS

Now working on the right side of the necklace, tie four linear series of double half hitch knots diagonally back and forth, as outlined on half hitch knot. Pull all of the strands under the top of the oval and then through and over the bottom of the oval, and position the oval about ¾" (2cm) from the last diagonal design element. Tie each of the 12 cords, one at a time, to the oval using double half hitch knots.

7. ESTABLISH SQUARE KNOT PATTERN

Gathering four cords at a time, tie eight rows of a loosely spaced alternating square knot pattern centered within the oval. (For the 1st row, square knot 1 and 4 around 2-3, 5 and 8 around 6-7, and 9 and 12 around 10-11. Then tie seven additional rows in the alternating square knot pattern.) When you've reached the bottom of the oval, secure each individual cord to the oval using a double half hitch knot.

8. BEGIN JOINING THREADS

Lay strand one across strands 2-6 at a steep diagonal and secure each of strands 2-6 individually to it with a double half hitch knot. (These knots should have a bit more space between them then the double half hitch knots tied at the top of the necklace.) Repeat on the other side by laying strand 12 across strands 7-

11 at a steep diagonal and securing each of strands 7–11 individually to it with a double half hitch knot.

9. CONTINUE DIAGONAL KNOTS AND COMPLETE WITH SQUARE KNOT

Lay what is now strand 1 (previously strand 2) across strands 2–6 at a diagonal parallel to the one above it and secure each of strands 2–6 to it with a double half hitch knot. Repeat with what is now strand 12 (previously strand 11) across strands 7–11 at a parallel diagonal to the one above it. Repeat this process once more on each side. Gather all the ends about 1" (3cm) below the bottom tips of the diagonal design elements in a large square knot, tying a double thickness of strands 1–2 and 11–12 around all the rest.

10. COMPLETE AND ADD CLASP

Finish this side of the necklace with a series of these chunky square knots spaced about 1" (3cm) apart until you've reached

a length even with the other side. Tie on the button to complete the clasp. Glue the knot, let it dry and trim the ends.

11. BEGIN DECORATIVE WIRE ELEMENT

With the 2' (61cm) length of 26-gauge silver-colored wire, start on the broad, outer edge of the large hoop portion of your necklace. Loop the end of the wire around the edge of the loop, leaving a small bit of a tail, and wrap the wire around the tail a few times to secure it to the loop. Tie the wire around the loop with eight half hitch knots. Wrap the wire tightly around the loop a few times, in the end, to secure it before trimming the ends.

12. ADD BEADS TO HOOP

Thread each of the seven labradorite beads of assorted small sizes onto a headpin and use your pliers to wrap the top of each headpin into a loop. Thread each one onto the outer edge of the wire coil created in the previous step before closing each loop with a secure wire wrap and trimming all the ends.

Tip:

Some beads available have holes that may not be large enough to accommodate your knotting material, so it's a good idea to bring samples of your cords with you when shopping for beads. If you just have to have something that has an

insufficient hole size, you may have to enlarge it. A bead reamer, also available at your local bead or craft stores, attached to a handheld power tool, may do the trick. Sometimes it's necessary to drill a larger hole using a cordless power tool, and a ¼" (6 mm) diamond hole saw drill bit in a small metal dish of water. The water keeps the crystal and the drill bit from getting too hot. Work slowly and be patient — it's a slow and steady process.

3.15. Metal Clay Josephine Bracelet

Our favorite single knot in macramé is the Josephine Knot. It's more complicated to tie than the others, and it's purely decorative. We love the look of the knot when tied with the rattail cord. If only it looked like that in metal. We have tried to work wire into the shape with no success.

So after much contemplation, we decided to translate the knot into the metal with metal clay. Metal clay is a malleable clay that is made up of microscopic particles of pure silver and organic materials. It can be molded and manipulated into many different shapes and forms. Here it takes the form of a Josephine knot using simple materials and cool tools.

About Metal Clay

Metal clay is a malleable clay that is made up of microscopic particles of pure precious metal (in this case, silver) and organic materials. It can be molded and manipulated into many different shapes and forms, decorated with textures and even embellished with lab-created stones or glass. (Everything you can do with it is far too extensive to cover in the pages of this book, but if you enjoy this project, we encourage you to explore it more on your own!) Once dry it's either fired in a kiln or — if the piece is small enough, like this one — fired by hand with a butane torch. In the firing process, the organic binders burn off, the piece shrinks slightly, and you're left with a piece of fine solid silver. Most quality bead and jewelry supply stores and many online retailers carry metal clay but are aware that there are a couple of different manufacturers, and the two types are not compatible, meaning they can't be combined. Metal clay has a tendency to dry out quickly if not properly handled, so you may want to first practice your designs with polymer clay, which has similar malleability but is less expensive and more readily available. Always study the manufacturer's instructions before working with polymer or metal clay.

Mod Knots

Josephine knot

Mod Materials

- a small amount of satin #2

- rattail cord for the knot template enough polymer clay to fit the rattail knot for the mold low-fire silver metal clay two medium amber dichroic glass beads

- Two extra small amber dichroic glass beads

- Two sections approximately 1½" (4cm) long sterling

silver,

- heavyweight link chain four 4" (10cm) 20g

- sterling silver wire sterling silver toggle clasp

- set of 2 stacked playing cards (three cards thick)

- olive oil water silver/black patina solution

- cotton swab

- steel wool

- round-nose pliers

- chain-nose pliers

- wire cutters

- craft knife emery board or small pieces of sandpaper in different grades brayer or small roller or piece of PVC pipe (about 6" [15cm])

- fire brick and tripod and metal screen metal clay work surface toaster oven for polymer clay butane torch and butane

- Dremel tool with a wire-bristle brush attachment

1. TIE JOSEPHINE KNOT FOR MOLD

Tie a large Josephine knot that will serve as the template for your mold. We used a rattail satin cord, but you can also experiment with other materials for different consistencies. Condition a small amount of polymer clay, roll it out, and lay the knot into the clay. Use a rolling pin or brayer to press the knot into the clay to make a good impression for the mold. (If you don't like the impression, simply knead it out and start over until you have a mold you like.) Bake the mold according to the manufacturer's instructions.

2. MOLD METAL CLAY INTO MOLD

Lubricate the work surface, your mold, your hands, and your tools that will be used with the metal clay with olive oil. Roll out the metal clay to a three-card thickness large enough to fit the mold, using the card stacks to assist. Press the clay into the mold evenly with a roller or brayer. Remove the clay from the mold and lay it on the lubricated work surface. Trim around the outside edge of the design with a craft knife. Poke holes in the ends where the wires will connect the silver piece to the bracelet. Let the clay dry thoroughly for a few hours. (Use any remaining clay as soon as possible or put it in an airtight container for later use, as it will dry out very quickly.)

3. SMOOTH EDGES BEFORE FIRING

Use an emery board or small piece of sandpaper to smooth the edges of the dry clay before firing the piece. It's very important that the piece be as smooth as possible. Check the holes to make sure they're clean and smooth. There is slight shrinkage when the clay is fired, so make sure the holes are big enough.

4. FIRE CLAY WITH BUTANE TORCH

Using a butane torch and working on a fireproof surface, fire the metal clay according to the manufacturer's instructions. Let it cool or quench it in water to speed up the cooling process.

Tip

To check if the metal clay is completely dry, slide it across your work surface. If it leaves a moisture trail, it needs more time. If there's no moisture trail, you're ready to do the finished work.

5. POLISH UNTIL SHINY

The fired metal clay has a white surface to it that needs to be burnished and then polished. Use a Dremel tool with a wire bristle attachment until the white finish has turned completely silver. The more you work the piece, the brighter it becomes.

6. ADD PATINA TO SILVER

Use a cotton swab to apply a bit of silver/black solution to the metal clay piece and to your lengths of chain, wire, and a clasp that will be used in this project. Rinse everything thoroughly with water and dry.

7. BUFF SURFACE WITH STEEL WOOL

Use the steel wool to buff off some of the black patina on the pieces. This leaves the

crevices and nooks and crannies dark and gives everything an antiqued feel.

8. ASSEMBLE BRACELET

Begin assembling one side of the bracelet in this order: Wire-wrapped loop, large bead, wire-wrapped loop, chain segment, wire-wrapped loop, a small bead, wire-wrapped loop, one half of toggle clasp. Repeat for the other side in the same order.

Chapter 4: Boho-Chic Patterns – Friendship Bracelets and Accessories

Bracelets knotted from the floss of the embroidery typically call to mind school and recess memories of the youth. However, by adding new colors and imaginative improvements to match your style, you can turn these styles from middle-school memories into modern items that you are proud to show. These designs will encourage you to create exactly what you want, whether you're going for a boho chic, retro, or all-out fashionista look. Start with the simple instructions for each pattern to learn how to arrange your threads, and the order to knot them to create your template and get the hang of things. Instead, take pleasure from the hundreds of ways you can tailor your designs and make them your own. There are countless options, from paint to closures to charms, to make these bracelets as special as you are!

4.1. French Twist or Chinese

STAIRCASE

You may construct an overall pattern known as a French Twist or Chinese Staircase, by using a repeated half-hitch knot. Start with seven 72 "(183 cm) strands doubled over for a total of fourteen strands. Use an overhand knot to tie the strands together with a 1/2" (1.5 cm) loop atop. Protect the work surface with the knotted end of the cuff.

1. Starting with your choice of colored thread, tie ten half hitch ties along the two threads. You may either use a knot forward or a knot backward (see this page), whichever is easier for you to construct.

2. Pick a different color string after you've done the first ten knots and use it to tie ten half-hitch knots around each other. Continue until the desired length is reached and alternate colors as you wish.

4.2. Three Stranded Braid

Start with three stranding groups. You may use anything from three 36 "(91.5 cm) single strands for a thin braid or doubled up six 72" (183 cm) strands or create a thicker braid of three four-strand sections.

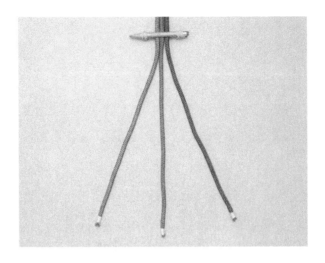

1. Tie the ends of the strands together by means of an overhand knot with a 1/2 "(1.5 cm) loop at the tip. Place the left group of strands over the middle strands such that the left group is in the middle. And bring the right group of strands over the center strands so that the right group is in the center.

2. Repeat until you achieve the desired amount. Bring a quick spin on this traditional style by increasing the number of strands you use and choosing matching colors. The top bracelet uses nine strands, the second two uses six strands and the bottom bracelet uses four strands.Small seed beads, shells, and bells make perfect embellishments for tiny braids. Make a full set of tons of colors that you can stack high on your wrist. Improve a simple braid by making a beaded focal section. Add beads to the outer strands as you braid them until the focal

section reaches the length you want.

4.3. Four-Strand Flat Braid

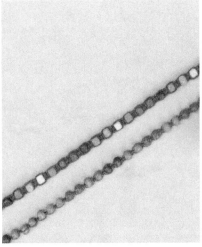

Start with two groups of 36 "(91.5 cm) strands. The pattern seen uses two groups of three strands together so you can use more or fewer strands in each group if you wish. 1 Fold one group of strands in half and tie an overhand knot with a 1/2" (1.5 cm) loop at the end. Thread through the loop the other pair of threads, then place them above the overhand knot. 2 Bring the outer right set of strands immediately to the left over the group. Continue on the outer left group of fibers, taking it straight to the right over the array. Bring the group center left over the group center-right. Hold the side of the thread by the side in each section as you work the braid. 3 Continue for new outer threads, in the middle of the ring, running the left group over the right side. Continue before the duration you like exceeds.Start with two 72 "(183 cm) strands doubled over for a total of four strands. 1 Arrange the strands to create the pattern you want. Make sure the outermost strands are two different colors to create a dual-color bracelet. Fasten the strands together using an overhand knot with a 1/2" (1.5 cm) loop at the top. 2 Bring the right outer strand under the center strands, and over the left outer strand. Bring the left outer strand over the center strands and under the right outer strand. 3 Bring the outer right strand over the middle strands and under the outer left strand to complete the square knot. Bring the left outer strand under the middle strands, then over the right outer strand. Repeat measures 2–3 before you get to the duration you like. ALTERNATING COLORS Use two strands of the same color for the outer strands and two strands of the same color for the internal strands to switch colors. Perform several knots in a square with the outer threads. Take the inner threads to the outside to turn colors, and deal on them some square knots. Arrange the threads so that the shades overlap to make a dual-color alternating bracelet. Bind several knots square to the outer strands. Take two threads of the same color to the outside to swap colors, and deal on them some square knots.

ADDING BEADS

Add small beads (like seed beads or 2 mm circular beads) when you tie the square knots to the outer working threads. Also, you can attach beads to one or both of the middle strands when working. Be creative on beads! Add small beads to each working strand, or thread the two working strands Make beads imaginative! To each working strand, add small beads, or loop all working strands into big beads, like the disk beads here. Add bright silver pin bling. Thread them on the two strands in the center. To make the silver pop, use bright, modern colors. Double over a baseline, to allow this pattern. Tie on two knotting strands in various colors. Tie knots only with a single color along the base string. Then, change to the second color. To build vibrant, colorful patterns, use the full colors of the rainbow! Create pretty flower patterns by threading a central bead on each outer strand to the two middle strands and three petal beads. This makes summer design perfectly casual.

4.4. Leather Lace Headband

Do store bought headbands ever give you a pressure headache? Not good. We are among those sufferers, but we like the look of headbands, so being the enterprising crafter that we are, we have always made our own.

This project uses square knots to tie some great natural leather lace, which will age nicely with time and use. Great stretchy material makes for a comfortable fit. Whoo hoo! It's so simple to make you could create one to match every outfit you own. Plus, this versatile knotting design can be easily adapted to create a bracelet, a belt or even a handcrafted strap for just about anything you can carry.

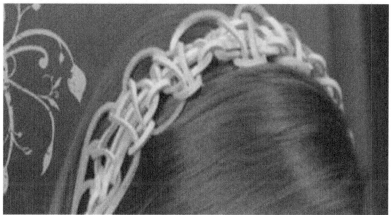

4.5. Wrapped-Ring Belt

This project is proof that necessity is the mother of invention. One of our friends was putting together an outfit and decided she needed a black belt, but it needed to be the kind that sits on the hips, which we didn't have. Using a large metal ring and the most wonderful black leather lace, we made her a belt. When we discovered the metal ring was the perfect size but not the most attractive belt buckle, wrapping the ring with leather lace seemed to be the answer. If you find yourself in the same situation, this belt can be whipped up in a flash to suit any outfit—just choose any colors and types of materials you'd like.

4.6. Mixed-Media Tie-Sash Belt

As you go shopping for materials to knot with, try looking for different types of cords that could create interesting effects when knotted together. Experiment with complementary colors in different materials, such as the rust colored rattail and copper leather lace used in this belt project. Combining various materials with different knots can result in pieces with beautifully interwoven textures and colors.

4.7. Leather And Suede Guitar Strap

When you are living your rock and roll fantasy, you play the bass guitar. So you need a strong, yet hip strap to hold our bass. Here we have combined macramé leather lace with super sturdy suede hide to create a functional yet stylish strap that will securely carry a heavy guitar. This strap is made using an adjustable strap as a pattern. You need to set the pattern to the size you like and that's how long your fancy strap will be. Your macramé strap won't be adjustable, but it will be really cool!

4.8. Your Best Friend's Collar and Leash

This project can work for either, but dogs seem to appreciate them more, while a cat kind of looks at you like you're crazy. So what else is new? We made this collar-leash combo with a big dog in mind, so we chose a really sturdy polypropylene cord as a base and accented it with thin turquoise leather lace for a little pop of color. Use a collar and leash that fits your dog well to calculate the lengths and also the hardware placement for this project.

4.9. Felted Ipod Cozy Pouch

This cute little bag is made by combining macramé with felting, a technique that is very popular with knitters.

Felting is the process of making an oversized wool item with the intention of washing and drying the fibers on high heat settings to compress and tighten them, giving the material a completely different, textural look. This bag begins with beautiful variegated Italian wool, and the felting process blends the colors for a unique look.

4.10. Hemp Yoga Mat

We can't help being one of those people that would rather make something we need than buy it. A holder for our yoga mat is just one of those things. Sturdy hemp makes a good strong frame, and brightly colored leather lace adds a pop of color. (Though you could opt for an entirely hemp project, or use another sturdy cord, like vegan-friendly ultra-suede, in lieu of the leather.)

Like the pouch on the previous pages, this project is created by "macramé in the round," working continuously by rotating the

136

piece and knotting the sides together on every other row. Try adapting this approach for bags of all sizes, from tiny amulet holders to big laundry sacks.

4.11. Drawstring Leather Purse

Leather lace is a great material to use for macramé belts and jewelry, but we really love using it for purses. This leather lace is soft and the color is bright and fun. It's the perfect material to use for this little drawstring bag that's just the right size for evenings or weekends, or anytime you simply don't need to carry too much stuff. At the bottom section of the bag, we'll be adding in some extra material, both for a design element and to increase the size. This project translates well to other sizes as well as different materials.

4.12. Chunky Wool Fringe Scarf

We have already mentioned our jealously of knitters and all the beautiful yarns they get to work with. We have to indulge in all of the hand-dyed, gorgeous wools and cottons and all of the other yummy yarns available.

If we can't knit them, we'll knot them! We chose some amazing handspun variegated wool yarn for this scarf. You need a lot of material to create such a big project, but trust me, the results are worth the indulgence.

4.13. Aloha Bamboo Handle Purse

These bamboo handles have a tropical feeling that reminds me of Hawaii. We needed to find just the right material to use to make this bag, and when we saw the cotton yarn — just the color of Hawaiian hibiscus flowers — we knew that was what it needed to be. Combining cool purse handles, soft, pretty yarn and interesting knot combinations, you get an awesome look-ing bag. We decided to add a suede pouch liner to keep your goodies hidden inside and provide a nice finished look — but your bag would be complete even without it.

Conclusion

Only several years ago, the fusion between art and fashion was formed entirely. We have now combined in a successful partnership that stimulates the creative expression of a new lifestyle. The word "Bohemian" has also been used to refer to the fashion and habits of poets, musicians, and other individuals who live outside of a particular society's norms and expectations. More recently, Bohemian chic evolved to the name "Boho-Chic," which is primarily influenced by nineteenth-century bohemian styles with some influences from modern fashion trends. It's a beautiful style that has made room for women in a variety of different fashions. Boho-Chic's apps are noteworthy in that they can produce some exact and special specifics about an ensemble of some kind of fashion is created. This style is one of today's most fascinating fashion trends, which takes a great sense of fashion to put together the right pieces to create an enviable and unique look. For this study, the fashion elements of this revival style are used in contemporary clothing designs that embody the Boho-Chic's aesthetic features in linking human beings with nature and the environment.

With this book, you will be able to explore various knots and techniques that are used for macramé. You can work by building up your skills as you go through each section, or simply dip in and out as you choose. Through step-by-step instructions, each technique was clearly outlined and demonstrated through photos and diagrams, making it simple for beginners. At the end of the book, there are fantastic tasks, outlined in step-by-step detail with 'you'll need' specifications, and there are even a few mini project ideas included so you can learn a technique and do it right away! Although the examples of the technique were worked with regular cords for maximum clarity, the project ideas illustrate how the simplicity of maximum visibility can be improved by picking various cords or strings, thicker or thinner, based on how you want to use the material. You'll also find out how adding beads will change the strategies for even more spectacular outcomes.

Printed in Great Britain
by Amazon